D1077625

MACGREGOR'S SCOTLAND
Macgregor Across Scotland
A LONG-DISTANCE WALK FROM MONTROSE TO ARDNAMURCHAN

JIMMIE MACGREGOR

BBC BOOKS

Published by BBC Books,
a division of BBC Enterprises Limited,
Woodlands, 80 Wood Lane, London W12 0TT

First published 1991

ISBN 0 563 36187 5

Set in 11 on 12pt Itek Bembo by Ace Filmsetting Ltd, Frome, Somerset
Printed and bound in England by Richard Clays Ltd, St Ives plc
Cover printed by Richard Clays Ltd, St Ives plc

'Macgregor Across Scotland' is a television programme produced by
Wildview Productions Limited for BBC Scotland

CONTENTS

ACKNOWLEDGEMENTS

MY THANKS GO once again to Dennis and Mary Dick of Wildview Productions for their meticulous preparation in the surveying of the route, and for the detailed planning required to move a film crew across the breadth of Scotland. Barry West and Bob Harle manhandled the camera and tape recorder into places where such machines were never meant to go. Our general factotum, Spike Flack, was as unfailingly helpful and good natured as he had been on the Southern Upland Way, and he was joined on this occasion by his father-in-law, Iain Murray, classics master turned carpenter and wood turner. In his 50s and several inches over 6 feet, Iain never looks as though he's hurrying, but covers hill ground at an alarming rate.

As ever, my great debt is to the many people along the way who gave unstintingly of their time and knowledge, adding yet a little more to my understanding of our country. Outstanding among these was Allan Mac Lachlan, piermaster at Kilchoan in Ardnamurchan, who gave me a well-reasoned and unemotional analysis of the effects of the rapid take-over of Scotland by outsiders.

A special word of appreciation must go to my friend and travelling companion, cartoonist Malky McCormick. Wherever I padded, Malky padded, often at a pace which I found quite challenging. There are two things which Malky does very well. He draws and he makes conversation. Both kept me vastly amused, on the hill and off.

PICTURE CREDITS

All photographs © Jimmie Macgregor

Cartoon by Malky McCormick

Map by Kate Simunek

THE AUTHOR

J IMMIE MACGREGOR is a graduate of the Glasgow School of Art, and has been, among other things, a schoolteacher, engraver, potter, naturalist, labourer, hospital porter, author, illustrator, folk musician, and radio and television presenter. He was deeply involved in the early days of the folk music revival in Britain and remained in the forefront of that movement for more than twenty years, becoming a household name through countless radio, concert and television appearances. He has toured the length and breadth of Britain many times, appearing in all kinds of venues from tiny folk clubs to the country's great theatres and concert halls, and his songs have taken him to Canada, Israel, the United States, Australia, Belgium, Holland, France, New Zealand, Germany, Austria, Russia and the Middle East.

Jimmie has made more than twenty long-playing albums, while several of his own songs and tunes have been used by fellow musicians, and he has composed and played theme music for radio and television. He has won an award for voice-over commentary on video, and his own highly successful daily radio programme, *Macgregor's Gathering*, on BBC Radio Scotland, has been running for more than eight years. The programme was granted a special prize by the Royal Society for the Protection of Birds, for its significant contribution to wildlife and conservation. Jimmie Macgregor has been made Scot of the Year by two separate organisations. He is a life member and vice-president of the Scottish Wildlife Trust, honorary vice-president of the Glasgow branch of the Scottish Youth Hostels Association, and President of Scottish Conservation Projects.

The BBC television series which inspired this book is the sixth in the *Macgregor's Scotland* series. The others are: *The West Highland Way, The Moray Coast, Speyside and the Cairngorms* (Speyside Way), *In the Footsteps of Bonnie Prince Charlie, On the Outer Edge* (remote Scottish islands), and *Along the Southern Upland Way*.

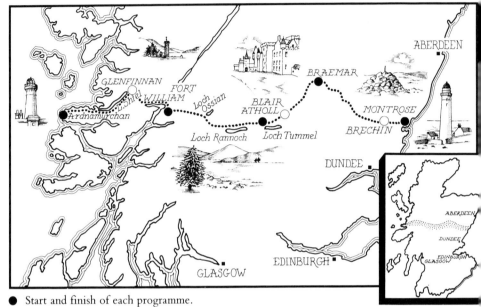

● Start and finish of each programme.
○ Other places en route.

INTRODUCTION

I T SEEMED LIKE a good idea at the time. Having discussed and discarded a number of concepts for our latest television series, producer Dennis Dick and I decided on a variation of my Southern Upland Way series which took me across the south of Scotland. This time I would go further north and begin at Montrose on the east coast. The lighthouse at Scurdie Ness would be my starting point, and I should finish by the Ardnamurchan light, at the most westerly point of the British mainland.

A minor snag immediately presented itself in the realisation that the lights were 370 kilometres apart. Furthermore, there was no recognised route. We decided to plot our own and go ahead. The journey proved to be among the most interesting I've undertaken and physically the most challenging. There were lots of ups and downs, mainly ups, sometimes as high as 900 metres. I negotiated forest tracks, waded rivers and, on occasions, had to seek out the faintest of ancient, near-forgotten rights of way. I took the track to the west by Shiel water and by Tummel and Loch Rannoch. I plodded the whole breadth of the Rannoch moor, to make my way through Glen Nevis beneath the giant bulk of the Ben. In a tiny boat I travelled the length of Loch Shiel, though in the opposite direction from that taken by Bonnie Prince Charlie when he came to raise his standard at Glenfinnan. There were wildlife reserves and visitors' centres, and I laid down my weary head in places as diverse as splendid hotels, a tent so small that I wore it rather than inhabited it, and a youth hostel where almost every imaginable function involved a bucket. The landscape and wildlife were endlessly interesting, my travelling companions were as affable and entertaining as they were professionally expert and, all in all, this was probably the most rewarding of my various walks for television.

Let me confess here and now that I did cheat once in a while. The mythical helicopter did not appear, but I used boats, ferries, and even a vintage steam train at one point. However, it was over the most demanding terrain that I legged it – the Rannoch Moor, Jock's Road – and I have the popped ligaments and eroded cartilages to prove it.

Scurdie Ness Lighthouse

SCURDIE NESS: INTROS AND OWNING UP

ROBERT STEVENSON was born in 1772, and when his widowed mother re-married, he found himself involved in his step-father's trade as a builder of lighthouses. He appears to have shown more than a little aptitude, for at the age of nineteen he supervised the erection of the light on the Wee Cumbrae and, at twenty-five, became engineer to the commissioners of northern lighthouses. He also masterminded the building of the light on the Bell Rock at the mouth of the Tay, a place which was a deadly hazard on a busy shipping route, claiming in the year of 1799, no less than 70 vessels. The rock disappeared under the tides to a depth of nearly 4 metres, and the work had to be carried out at frantic speed. Huge stones were precisely cut on shore to be fitted when the rock was exposed. Robert's career went from strength to strength and when he died in 1850, his sons were well established. Thomas and David were the builders of the tower at Scurdie Ness. Robert Louis Stevenson, Thomas's son, had a fancy for quite a different trade.

The area between Bell Rock and Girdle Ness was notorious for shipwrecks, and the little seafaring community of Ferryden had long seen the need for a lighthouse, but it wasn't until 1870 that the light at Scurdie Ness shone for the first time, to the great delight of the fisherfolk cheering on the shore. The brilliantly white tower stands 39 metres high, and before the light became automated, those with sufficient puff and muscle power could climb the 170 steps to the top for a tremendous view over Angus and the Mearns, and on a clear day, all the way down the coast to Berwick.

During the Second World War, the lighthouse became an object of disagreement between our armed forces. The navy needed the light, and the air force wanted it shut down, as it led the German bombers in. One unfortunate keeper had to paint the whole huge structure black so that it did not provide an obvious landmark in daytime.

It has been my experience on these jaunts around Scotland that whenever we set up the camera in a village street or other populous place, there is always someone who will say, with many a nod and wink, 'There you are. I always said he wasn't alone on these walks. In fact, I was just saying to Mrs Johnson in number 27 that there *must* be people with him on that mountain.' I always congratulate these people on their perspicacity, and on this occasion I decided that my

11

(*Left*)
Ferryden

(*Page 13*)
The Montrose Basin

opening piece to camera at Scurdie Ness would include an intro-
duction on film of Malky McCormick and the whole crew. Yes,
you've guessed it: Barry, our cameraman, couldn't be on film, but we
got him into the publicity shots.

Having informed the viewers of what I was about, Malky and I set
off along the pleasant cliff path to the wee village of Ferryden. The
day was fine, flowers were blooming, sea birds were calling, and
Malky was talking. Malky continued talking for 370 kilometres, but
his enthusiasm was infectious and we were already enjoying
ourselves.

A glance at the map will show that Ferryden and Montrose face
each other across a narrow inlet from the North Sea, and from the village it's clear that the harbour is bustling and busy, with craft of all
shapes and sizes coming and going. This activity has been continuous
since the thirteenth century, for among the many east-coast
communities which carried on a long and prosperous trade with the
Baltic, Montrose was pre-eminent. As with so many places on the
North Sea, oil now rules. Our route was to bypass Montrose, but I had
visited it several times in my itinerant folk-singing days and knew it
well as an attractive and interesting place. Its main street is one of the
widest I've seen anywhere. It is now divided into two one-way sys-
tems, which is very sensible, but turn off, and you find yourself in a
maze of wynds and closes, with little houses set in secluded gardens
and yards. If you add to all this a fabulous beach and miles of sand
dunes, with your own vast nature reserve, you have not a bad place in
which to live. It even has its own tame artist, James Morrison, an old
friend and fellow student at the Glasgow School of Art, and now
doing very well indeed, thank you.

MUD, MOLLUSCS AND MAGIC

L EAVING MONTROSE, I was interested to pass the proposed site of the Scottish Wildlife Trust's new visitors' centre at Rossie Braes, but what I was really looking for was a gigantic bowl of clabber*: a vast, brackish dub* known as the Montrose Basin. As the tide comes in through the narrow channel from the North Sea, salt water mixes with the South Esk river and gradually, countless little gullies, ditches, runnels and potholes fill up, until the whole 800 hectares of mud and sand is covered by a huge inland loch. The surface can be covered by roosting birds, but it's when the waters recede that the place comes into its own. A huge oozing mud flat is exposed which harbours a myriad small, burrowing, creeping, swimming, wriggling and jumping life forms: a gourmet's delight for the swans, ducks, divers and waders, with the ever-present piratical crows and gulls. These last even feed upon the feeders, and it's a lucky duck that doesn't see some of her offspring disappear down the gaping maw of one of the huge black-backs.

The Montrose Basin is an official wildlife reserve and I had arranged to meet the Scottish Wildlife Trust's ranger, Rick Goater, who has the demanding task of looking after the whole area. Rick had some very useful information for me and I was green with envy when he told me that on a single day his list of predators seen hunting over and around the basin had included osprey, sparrowhawk, kestrel, merlin, short-eared owl and peregrine. The amount of food produced

in the ooze is quite extraordinary. There is a little mud snail which grazes the algae, and 36 000 have been counted within one square metre. It has been calculated that in the Montrose Basin as a whole, this represents a banquet of 75 000 kilos of snails. Add garlic and butter and you have an impressive dish. There are certain wildlife enthusiasts who get quite excited about doing this kind of calculation. I'm not one of them, but I am impressed to learn that something in the order of 200 000 kilos of animal protein is produced each year in the Montrose Basin.

It's small wonder that the reserve attracts birds in their thousands. Rick walked around with me and pointed out that the reserve also includes surrounding areas of salt marsh, which support around 3000 wigeon. There are also plenty of trees, scrub and dry grassland, providing nesting and feeding places for a wide variety of species. Even on the mud flats, feeding methods vary, the long-billed waders probing deep in the mud for worms and shrimps, the eider ducks tearing off mussels and swallowing them shells and all, mallard and shelduck sieving the mud through plates in their bills, trapping worms, shrimps and tiny shellfish.

I was delighted, as I always am, to see swans with healthy cygnets, and Rick told me that the reserve supports 200, together with 2000 redshank, and 35 000 pink-footed geese. Figures like these make the Montrose Basin an internationally important reserve. It is also a beautiful and endlessly fascinating place, and it's good news for all wildlife enthusiasts that it's in the hands of the Scottish Wildlife Trust and looked after by a ranger as enthusiastically committed as Rick Goater. Even those with no more than a passing interest in wildlife would enjoy a visit to the Montrose Basin, and further information can be had from the Scottish Wildlife Trust, 25 Johnston Terrace, Edinburgh.

With a combination of low tides and hot days, the basin can sometimes begin to smell a little high, and it's not everyone who can rhapsodise about a sea of gunge. However, if you spend a day here surrounded by teeming life, watch huge, cacophonous flights of geese winging in, or marvel as the lumbering take-off of a family of mute swans is transformed into glorious, powerful flight, you will begin to feel that there is magic here.

---

* *clabber* = mud   * *dub* = puddle

STONES, STEAM AND A
CHOO-CHOO BOW-WOW

ALKY WAS ALREADY enthusing about the hills rising in the distance before us and was all for pressing on, but as we glimpsed the distant House of Dun on the main Brechin road, I remembered that on my daily radio programme, *Macgregor's Gathering*, I had interviewed architect James Simpson about the house and its builder, William Adam. James, who works on the restoration of historic buildings, told me that it was said of Adam that he 'acquired a handsome fortune with an unspotted character'. Not an easy thing to do, but William Adam achieved much more, although his reputation was overshadowed by that of his brilliant and famous sons, James, William, John and, especially, Robert. Their father's reputation has been re-assessed, and he is now given great credit for his development and refinement of the Palladian style of architecture which has given Scotland so many superb buildings.

William Adam was born in 1689. His father was a Kirkcaldy stonemason and William followed the same trade. After travelling abroad, he became involved in many business ventures, involving coal, salt, land, milling, brewing and agriculture. In all of these, his energy and creativity brought considerable rewards. His burgeoning talent as an artist and architect was underpinned by a solid understanding of building techniques, but it is as a wonderfully creative designer that he is best remembered, having put his signature on some of Scotland's finest houses: Haddo, Tinwald, Craigdarroch and Mellerstain, among others.

The House of Dun was built for the Erskine family who were traditionally the Lairds of Dun and it demonstrates not only Adam's unerring grasp of scale and proportion, but also his attention to detail. He oversaw everything from the most massive façades to the smallest features of furnishing and plasterwork. The landscaping around the house was also his work, and the gardens and grounds, like the house, are open to the public. All is now in the care of the National Trust for Scotland who have done a wonderful job in restoring and maintaining the House of Dun, a magnificent example of Scottish architecture, and the work of William Adam.

As we crossed the Bridge of Dun with its ornate pillars and little inset pedestrian galleries, we noticed a column of smoke and a puff of

steam rising from the station, a few hundred metres distant. We knew there was a vintage steam railway at Bridge of Dun, but hadn't realised that it was operational, though only on test runs. Malky shamelessly suggested that we might scrounge a lift into Brechin, if no one was looking. I equally shamelessly told him that I couldn't be less concerned who was looking, and we broke into an eager trot. By sheer good luck, Max Maxwell and Katrina Ballantyne who live at the station and look after the buildings and rolling stock, were about to make a test run, and invited us along.

Coaches and engines stood around in various stages of dilapidation and restoration. The whole complex is in the care of a group of dedicated steam railway buffs who make up the Brechin Railway Preservation Society. Iain Smith looks after publicity, while Ian Laird plays guard. The level of commitment is well demonstrated by the fact that the fireman, Steve Pegg, maintained his routine railway duties throughout the year of his final medical examinations. He passed. These were the people I had the good fortune to meet, but they can call on a wide range of supporters when the need arises.

Malky and I agreed that the star of the group was Filou. For all the sophistication of the name, Filou is an attractively scruffy raggedy wee dog, looking like a lavatory brush which has just been plugged

(*Left*)
Bridge of Dun

(*Right*)
Max with Filou

into an electric socket. Filou is the French for Fido, and means scamp or rascal, though I must say that, unlike some small dogs, Filou was remarkably un-yappy and hysterical. She was also a steam-railway enthusiast.

I climbed up on to the small and bakingly hot foot-plate and with Max at the controls, and Dr Steve Pegg displaying considerable skill with the coal shovel, we set off for Brechin. As we moved off, Filou leapt from the platform to establish herself on her regular wooden platform above the coal box. She seemed perfectly happy and relaxed, poised over the edge, as we rumbled and jolted along on a steep bank above the fields. She lost her composure only once, when she spotted a hare making its way along the edge of a field far below, and I had to grab a handful of spiky hair to prevent a flying Filou launching herself into space.

The Brechin Railway Preservation Society has already done a fine job in restoring the old station at Bridge of Dun, and in addition to some lovely antique coaches, they have six steam engines and seven or eight diesels. At the time of writing they were open to the public on Sundays only, but plan to extend these hours by 1991 and to push on with the restoration of the station at Brechin.

BRECHINS AND CATERTHUNS, COUGHS AND SNEEZES

A S WE EMERGED from the station into St Ninian's Square, I realised that although I had performed in Brechin several times in my folk-singing days, it was a place which I really didn't know. One always seemed to be driving through it on the way to somewhere else. Even that has changed, since the town is now bypassed by the A94. A pity really, for it's a place of some interest and considerable antiquity.

In the 1700s and 1800s, Brechin had developed as the centre of traditional hand-loom weaving in the area and several very successful factories had been set up. As well as the textile industry, there was also engineering and distilling, the latter being the only one left of Brechin's older trades, though several new ventures are under way, notably meat processing and the canning of fruits and vegetables.

Brechin's cathedral no longer has a bishop, but it has a history going back to around AD 900, when it was founded by Irish evangelists. The building has served several religious denominations in the course of its long history and has played host, sometimes unwillingly, to many great names. Founded by King Kenneth in the year 971, it was knocked about a bit by Cromwell in 1653. In 1746, Bonnie Prince Charlie dropped in, closely followed by his arch enemy and conqueror, the Duke of Cumberland.

The grand castle in Brechin is the home of the Earl of Dalhousie, through whose estates I should be walking. It was in Brechin Castle that Balliol handed over the Kingdom of Scotland to the English in 1296, one of the few historical facts to remain in my head since my schooldays. It was here too that the Earl of Dalhousie's courageous but indiscreet ancestor, Sir Thomas Maule, was flattened by a huge catapulted stone during a siege by Edward I.

Our progress towards the Angus hills took us through the village of Little Brechin; a very well cared-for wee place, but don't walk too quickly or you'll miss it. So far, all the walking had been on the flat, but we soon found ourselves on a modest slope on a good path which took us to one of two hill forts in the area. They are known as the White Caterthun and the Brown Caterthun. The sites are in the care of the Scottish Development Department (Historic Buildings and Monuments section) who have erected a notice which reads:

Southesk Church, Brechin

The Brown and White Caterthuns are heavily defended hilltop settlements of the Iron Age, some 2000 to 2500 years old, although they are of different types and were probably occupied at different times. 'Brown' and 'White' refer to the heather-covered turf and stone ramparts of one, and the massive, collapsed stone rampart which is the main feature of the other.

The Brown Caterthun has six lines of defence, probably reflecting three or four phases of construction and use. There are numerous entrances through the ramparts.

(*Above*) Roadside sign, Little Brechin   (*Page 21*) On the Caterthun

The White Caterthun is also a fort of considerable complexity. Four lines of defence survive. The innermost is the best preserved and the most easily visible. One rampart can only be detected on aerial photographs. Two or three phases may be represented.

Impressive stuff, but in places like this, I am always less persuaded by historical and archaeological detail than by the sense of timelessness and the feeling of being directly connected to people who went before. They hunted, toiled and fought here; lived their brief lives and disappeared, but their presence lives on in the stones.

Even at the modest elevation of the forts, the views were extensive on this bright, breezy day. To the north-east lay the Howe o' the Mearns. Before us spread the low, rolling ground of Strathmore, like

a contour map, with the chequered pattern of the agricultural land punctuated by the exotic golden patches of oil-seed rape. Rape was a crop fed to livestock until someone realised the value of the seeds for the manufacture of cooking oils and margarines. It is now probably the most profitable crop in Scotland, and the beautiful, subtle colours of ripening corn, oats and barley are rudely shouted down by raucous chrome yellow.

Oil-seed rape is a controversial crop in more ways than its aesthetic effect on the landscape. More and more people are complaining that the pollen from the yellow flowers causes great discomfort, in the form of various allergies and symptoms similar to those of influenza. The scientists are taking the complaints seriously enough to investigate them, but at the time of writing, nothing has been proven. The farmers dismiss the worries as nonsense and tell us that the pollen from the rape flower is carried only by insects and is not wind borne at all. Those living near the fields are unimpressed and continue to sniff and snuffle their complaints.

Behind us, to the north-west, we could pick out some of the peaks of the Cairngorm mountains, with an enticing glint of distant snow. Malky was restless and eager to get to the higher ground so, turning our backs on the distant spires of Montrose, the strath and the sea, we headed for Glen Lethnot and over to Glen Esk.

WHO'S RIGHT?

A PLEASANT and fairly easy walk took us to the Stonyford Bridge across the West Water, where we came across our first 'Right of Way' sign. These signs, and the rights of way they indicate, are now quite jealously guarded by outdoor people of many kinds, who see them under threat as never before. They were of crucial importance to the old country way of life, and some have been used by many generations. The old hill tracks were used by the cattle drovers, as whisky or coffin trails, or were simply the connecting links between communities. When the industrial revolution created great surplus wealth in the south, with increased leisure for the well-heeled, it became the fashion to acquire an estate in Scotland. The sheep which had supplanted the people in the Highland clearances were taken off the hill to create huge tracts of land which became sporting playgrounds for the wealthy. The new Victorian landowners frequently attempted to deny people access by closing off the traditional rights of way. Many battles were fought in the courts, and sometimes out of them, to secure the ways for the people.

Since that time there has been an unstated agreement that responsible people have a right of free access to the Scottish countryside. However, the belief, often loudly promulgated in the pub, that there is no law of trespass in Scotland, is wishful thinking. What has developed is a mutual tolerance and understanding, but a landowner is legally entitled to take action in the case of damage or disruption. This system has been working pretty well for some time, with most estate owners understanding the need to enjoy the open spaces, and most outdoor folk being genuinely concerned for the countryside. There is, however, a new threat in the number of estates being bought up by people from other countries, with no understanding or concern for these traditional agreements. 'This is mine, keep out,' is the message, reinforced by gates, padlocks, and unsympathetic hirelings. The attitude is reprehensible, but quite legal. Somehow, I can't see the Scots standing for much of this, and there's probably trouble brewing.

At the risk of preaching, I must say that we strengthen our own case by taking care not to disrupt the business of the countryside. In my experience, people who work in the country – the ghillies, shepherds, estate managers – are decent, friendly folk who will co-operate with anyone who is being sensible.

Don't go shouting and bawling around the hills, and don't leave rubbish behind you. If you find a gate closed, close it after you. If it has been left open, you leave it open too. Don't disturb livestock. A shepherd is quite entitled to shoot your dog if it attacks or harries his animals. Keep it on a lead or leave it at home. These are common-sense rules, but you should be aware of the activities of the estates.

Everyone knows that the grouse season starts on 12 August. Make sure that it's not the hiker season too. Keep away from areas where you might flush birds in the wrong direction, or the right direction, depending on your point of view. Grouse shooting goes on until 10 December, but August is the month to worry about.

Red deer stags are shot on the hill from the beginning of July until 20 October, and the hinds from 21 October until 15 February. No one would suggest that you stay off the hills during the whole of this period, but you should be aware of what's going on and, if in doubt, a call to the estate office could be useful.

THE CLASH, THE KNOCK
AND THE MONARCH

THE OLD PATH from the Stonyford Bridge is known as the Priest's Road, and winds its way over the hill to Glen Esk. We were hill walking at last, and as we stopped to consult the map by the Clash of Wirren, we saw that we were surrounded by equally ear-tickling place names. Ahead was West Knock, while below us was the Water of Saughs (Willows). To the north we could pick out Sturdy Hill, the Hill of Fingray, Mount Battock, Mulnabracks, the Hill of Cat, Cock Cairn and Braid Cairn: a ring of hills between 610 and 760 metres, except Mount Keen, at over 914 metres, still carrying some snow this far into the summer.

The day was fresh, the pull up wasn't too heavy, and all the way there were frequent sightings of mountain hares, deer, and the ever-present red grouse. It was almost with regret that we commenced the descent to Glen Esk, where a meeting had been arranged with Dalhousie Estate factor, Richard Cooke, and Fred Taylor, the head stalker in Glen Esk. Richard feels that the Dalhousie Estate takes an enlightened view of estate management and does everything possible to co-operate with those wishing to explore and enjoy the country-

Fred Taylor and Richard Cooke

side. At the car park at Invermark, a display board has been set up offering photographs and useful information on the local wildlife and general rules for the protection of the countryside.

Both Richard and Fred feel that problems are on the increase. There are more deer on the hills, which means more time spent in necessary culling, but there are more people on the hill too, and the growing hobby of Munro bagging means that the deer are now being disturbed in the most remote corries and glens, making management much more difficult. A Munro is a mountain of over 914 metres and is named after the man who first went out and actually measured them. Richard's policy is to give people as much information and advice as possible, and hope they'll act on it. A hard day, or even a whole weekend, of stalking and manoeuvring deer into a specific area, can be spoiled by one thoughtless walker or climber.

The red deer is our largest wild mammal, and one that commands much admiration. There are few finer sights than a herd posing on the skyline, and one of the most stirring sounds on the hills is the primeval challenging roar of a rutting stag. The image of the stag was ennobled forever by Edwin Landseer in his famous painting *Monarch of the Glen*, but many of the animals now seen on the hill look rather less than regal. The problem is that there are just too many of them. The plan for 1990 was to remove about 50 000 from the overall estimated population in Scotland of 300 000. No more than a step in the right direction, as deer experts calculate that the Scottish hills should be supporting no more than 150 000 beasts. There isn't enough food to support any more animals in good health, and even the casual walker with a pair of glasses can observe that many deer look thin and undersized.

The massive fourteen-pointer trophy heads displayed on the walls of hotels and pubs are likely to be forest animals from Germany, and indeed our own deer used to be a forest animal in the days of the great Caledonian forests. With more shelter and a better food supply, it was undoubtedly once a bigger and stronger beast – the natural prey of the wolf and earlier possibly also the bear. Even now, the deer which live in the mixed, open forest of Glen Trool is a considerably heftier species. The deer's only enemy today is man, with his continued exploitation of the animal's natural habitat, and as land is fenced off or degraded by over-grazing, the deer become a nuisance to agriculture and forestry.

The essential culling of red deer has been a routine seasonal activity in the Scottish highlands for a very long time, contributing not only to the economy of the estates, but to the long-term welfare of the deer population. Controlling the stags is relatively simple. It is also profitable, as there are many people who will pay handsome sums for a day's stalking on the Scottish hills, with a trophy at the end of it. On the hill, the head stalker's word is law, and anyone who demonstrates insufficient skill to make a clean shot, or who appears trigger-happy, will be taken off without hesitation.

The control of red deer hinds presents a real problem. They are culled much later than the stags, from October until February, and it's not quite so easy to persuade people to pay a lot of money to spend a long day on a frozen mountain in the hope of bagging an animal which doesn't even have antlers to show off on the wall. The estates have to reduce the numbers themselves and with the number of estate employees greatly diminished, it becomes a laborious and expensive exercise when venison prices are low. The result is that many deer die a slow death by starvation in hard winters. Anyone who has come across these emaciated carcases, or seen a weakened animal staggering around on buckling legs while the hoodie crows gather, will appreciate that a clean shot at the onset of winter is a welcome alternative.

It's undoubtedly the handsome spread of antlers which gives the red deer stag the title 'Monarch of the Glen'. Remarkably, these huge growths are produced and shed every year, representing a colossal output of energy and material. The animals often eat the fallen antlers to re-cycle the calcium they contain. There are stags which, for some reason, do not grow antlers. These are called hummel stags. (In Scotland, gloves without fingers are known as hummel-doddies.) Although the hummels may be a bit pansy looking, they tend to be bigger and heavier and in the competition of the rut, get more than their fair share of the action with the hinds.

MALKY, THE MONSTER AND LOCH BRANDY

TAKING OUR LEAVE of Richard Cooke and Fred Taylor in Glen Esk, a short walk took us past the ancient castle of Invermark, and on to Kirkton and the old church and graveyard at the eastern end of Loch Lee. This is a still, lonely and beautiful spot, but we paused only long enough for me to take some photographs and for Malky to knock off a couple of sketches.

Malky had been drawing steadily since we started off, working from a little sketching kit he carried in a plastic map case. I was always interested to observe the reactions of the subjects of his caricatures. Some are perceptive enough to recognise that he has pinpointed their

Invermark Castle

salient features. Many are taken aback, and a characteristic reaction is, 'Oh yes, very nice; but surely I don't have a double chin?' This is quite likely to come from someone with an array of chins cascading down to the navel like a dangling accordion. However, as Malky points out, they all want to keep their portraits, have them signed, and in all probability, framed and hung in a very prominent place.

The track along the 7 kilometres or so of Loch Lee was flat, pleasant going, but when we got to Inchgrundle at the far end of the waters, things changed. By a beautiful grove of larch trees we found a sign which said simply, 'CLOVA: The Scottish Rights of Way Society'. We quickly discovered that this was all the information we were getting about the path for Glen Clova, which rose steeply around the wood and virtually disappeared. A quick scout around, however, and a look at the map and we were back on course. Malky was all for going straight ahead up the Shank of Inchgrundle, but the map indicated a steep, broken ascent, and I suggested that we skirt around the edge, and up over Skulley and Wester Skulley. The day was fresh and cool, with dry, hard going underfoot; ideal for the long plod up the rounded bulk of the Muckle Cairn. The Muckle Cairn is one of those big, sprawling, rather featureless hills where one plods on and on without appearing to get any closer to the summit, so we were intrigued to have the monotony broken by the appearance of a prehistoric monster creeping along the skyline.

The monster, as it edged nearer, turned out to be one of those many-wheeled overland vehicles. They go slowly, but almost anywhere, and save a great deal of wearisome leg work on rough ground. They have, in many areas, replaced the Highland garrons – the sturdy ponies which used to bring deer carcases off the hill. The man at the wheel was an affable character called Sandy Mearns. Sandy is a big, robust man, and his colleague, equally sturdy looking, rejoices in the name of Sherard Hubbert. The monster is known as an ATV, an all-terrain vehicle, and when Sandy offered us a lift to the top of the hill, we had no hesitation in chucking the gear in the back and climbing aboard. The ride over the broken ground was almost as tiring as walking, but the aches and pains were in different places. We had a brief break for a bite and a drink with Sandy and Sherard and I noticed once again that these professional outdoor men eschew the fancy modern gear and stick to tweeds. Both were wearing the estate tweed, but Sandy told me that, good though it was, it wasn't up to the standard of the older cloths. 'As a matter of fact,' he said, 'you could read the *Dundee Courier* through it.'

At the summit of the Muckle Cairn at about 750 metres, we left the ATV and made our way across to Loch Brandy. The curving head of Loch Brandy is cupped by a most impressive horseshoe-shaped cliff dropping sheer to the water. My producer, Dennis Dick, was interested in a distant shot of Malky and me on the edge of the cliff, so off we went, while Barry West set up his camera. There was a steep descent before the climb back up, and halfway down I spotted a potentially good camera shot along the cliff face. To save time, I asked Malky to extract the camera from my pack. I took my pictures, and when I turned, Malky was gone. By the time I had taken off my pack, replaced the camera and buckled up again, Malky was halfway to the top, leaving me puffing up behind. However, Dennis did eventually get his shot of the two tiny figures dwarfed by the scale of the cliff.

Pausing long enough on the cliff edge to take in the view of Loch Brandy, and the silver thread of the river South Esk snaking away along Glen Clova, we made the steep, knee-jolting descent known as the Snub. A brief stop at the Clova Inn, where we were made most welcome, saw us suitably refreshed for the walk along to the youth hostel at Glendoll.

The Clova Sign

GLENDOLL, JOCK'S ROAD
AND DAVY'S BOURACH

THE YOUTH HOSTEL at Glendoll Lodge is very attractive and comfortable, and is presided over by warden John Jones, who turned out to be an old friend of a friend, one Dom Capaldi who ran the hostel at Rattigan. There were few hostellers in residence on the night that we stayed, so John had time to relax, talk, and have his portrait done and presented by Malky.

Youth hostels were very important to me in my early outdoor days, and later, when I was a student, I served some time as an assistant warden at the splendid Auchendennan hostel on Loch Lomond. The Scottish Youth Hostels Association does a fine job in supplying cheap, basic accommodation in sometimes quite out of the way places. Things have changed greatly since I was a lad, and mainly for the better. Many of the hostels now supply covered duvets, an idea which would have had us all falling about laughing at one time. The hostel shops are bigger and better stocked, and the buildings are generally better cared for. Some of the old-timers are deeply offended by what they see as a sissifying process, but most hostellers are grateful for the improved services.

The stretch from Glendoll to Braemar would be the most taxing so far, but we were looking forward to it as an especially interesting part of the walk. The first couple of miles are through the dense Glendoll forest, but one soon emerges into open country, and the uphill slog is on again. This is a very famous right of way which was nearly lost when an estate owner tried to close it off about 100 years ago. He was confronted by the Scottish Rights of Way Society and wound up in court, where it was proved that the route through Glendoll had been in common use for a very long time.

The track is known as Jock's Road and it was only when the case went on to the House of Lords that the derivation of the name was explained. At one time Lord Invercauld and Lord Aberdeen were contesting ownership of the land traversed by the pass. A witness in the case related the story of an ancestor who, with a group of friends, confronted Lord Aberdeen on the path and forced him to turn back. Lord Aberdeen was a powerful and influential man unused to such treatment and was irritated enough to offer a reward for the apprehension of the ringleader, one John Winter. John took refuge for

Glendoll Hostel

some time in a shepherd's hut in the glen, and the route has been known as Jock's Road ever since.

Wildlife is not one of Malky McCormick's special interests, but he is an enthusiast in all things and a keen observer of everything around him. He was struck by the number of hares scattering in every direction on the hill above us. This was quite a different animal from the brown hare of the lowlands. The mountain or blue hare is much darker along the back with the blue-grey colour of its lighter parts giving it its second name. The mountain hare is an animal which can survive where no brown hare could manage. The pads of the hind feet are spread and hairy to give protection and grip in snow and in winter the hare changes its coat for a camouflaged pelt of pure white. Because the animal is at the southern edge of its territory, it is sometimes caught out in glaringly white livery when the snows have gone, making it an easy target for the eagle and hill fox.

Davy's Bourach

With the ribbon of the White Water far below and the hill rising steeply on our right, we padded steadily upward to emerge through a narrow pass approaching a hill called Cairn Lunkard. Just off the path to the left is a mountain shelter known as Davy's Bourach. Bourach is possibly a corruption of the old Scots word, bourie, meaning an animal's den. In the south of Scotland, a bourach is a shepherd's hut, and as a verb the word means to enclose. It certainly doesn't mean anything too posh, for Davy's Bourach is a pretty basic affair, built into the hillside with a dry-stone front wall, a roof of timbers covered over with corrugated iron and a layer of heather turf.

The Bourach is in memory of an old friend of mine called Davy Glen. A likable, stocky character with a flowing white beard, Davy was a kenspeckle* figure on the Scottish hills for many a year. He was deeply interested in Scottish history and tradition; he had the kind of knowledge of wildlife which is only gained in the field, and he was a keen photographer and amateur artist. He met my son Gregor only once, when he was a toddler, but every year until he died he sent Gregor a birthday present of one of his little hand-carved and painted wooden medallions. His best gift to me was a version of the song *The Laird o' Cockpen*, which is very different to the one I learned at school.

---

* *kenspeckle* = well-known, familiar

THE LAIRD O' COCKPEN
Davy Glen's version

The Laird o' Cockpen, he's puir and he's duddy,
Wi' drinkin' and daffin' his heid is aye muddy;
But noo he's determined tae tak a bit wife,
Gin she should torment him the rest o' his life.

At the back o' the knowe this body did dwell,
For muckin' the byre he thocht she'd do well;
McLeish's ae dochter, 'though blin' o' an e'e,
And canna brag muckle o' her pedigree.

His wig was weel kaimed and pouthered wi' meal,
Says he tae hinsel' 'I'm a gey spruce bit cheil.'
His waistcoat was red, and his breeks were plush blue,
Wi' a great hole ahint where his sark tail hung through.

His hoose, 'though but sma', was plenished fu' weel,
And wi' plenty o' whisky he cared no' the de'il.
White puddin's weel flavoured wi' pepper and saut,
Sae wha' could refuse the Laird wi' a' that.

He's mounted his cuddy and cantered away,
Until that he cam' tae the end o' the brae;
'Gae tell Mistress Jean tae come tae the hoose end,
For she's wanted tae speak tae the Laird o' Cockpen.'

Mistress Jean she chanced tae be feeding the swine;
'What the de'il brings the body at sic' a like time?'
So she thumpit and grumpit and garred them stan' roon,
Syne kilted her coaties and cam' awa' doon.

And when the Laird saw her he bobbit fu' low,
And said he was come for tae mak' her his Jo.
'I'll just hae a word wi' ma auld Mither, ken,
And faith I'll go with ye this nicht tae Cockpen.'

The Laird started up and took Meg by the hand,
The auld wife consented, sae did the auld man.
Mess John said the blessing, and bade them guid sen,
And aye tae be fruitfu' and plenish Cockpen.

They mounted the cuddy and awa' they did ride,
And happier never were bridegroom and bride,
And 'though they had nocht but a but and a ben,
Maist ance every year comes an heir tae Cockpen.

Duddy = ragged; *daffin'* = carousing; *gin* = if, although; *knowe* = small hill; *muckin' the byre* = cleaning the cowshed; *ae* = only, single, one; *muckle* = big, great, a lot; *kaimed and pouthered* = combed and powdered; *breeks* = trousers; *ahint* = behind; *sark* = shirt; *cuddy* = horse; *brae* = hill; *garred* = made; *kilted her coaties* = hitched up her skirts; *bobbit* = bowed; *Jo* = sweetheart; *Mess John* = the minister; *sen* = luck; *but and ben* = back and front rooms.

HIGH POINT

A LITTLE WAY ON from Davy's Bourach is a stark reminder of the dangers in the Scottish hills. Pinned to a rock on the right of the track is a plaque in memory of a group of walkers who lost their lives here. These were not casual ramblers, but people well acquainted with the hills. They were making the same trip as we were, but in the opposite direction and in severe conditions, when they became separated and disorientated. All succumbed to exhaustion and exposure, one of the group dying within yards of the potentially life-saving shelter of the Bourach. In March 1976, two girls died in the same area in the same way.

It cannot be overstressed that conditions change quite dramatically with the seasons. The topography is not constant, prominent land-marks disappearing and deep treacherous gullies filling up with wind-driven snow. The real danger is in the winter, but even at other times mist, wind and rain can cause confusion and, ultimately, dangerous fatigue and exposure.

The question of safety on the hills has been touched on elsewhere in the *Macgregor's Scotland* series (especially in *On the West Highland Way*), but it is one that can bear repetition. The most important thing is to avoid underestimating the hazards. This is a mistake often made by visitors from other countries. They look at a map and think, '1300 metres? Ben Nevis? That's nothing compared to a modest Alp or Rocky!' They forget that in this country, one person can be wandering around at sea level in a T-shirt and shorts, while 600 or 700 metres above, someone else is battling in near-Arctic conditions. At Inversnaid some years ago, a tall, distinguished-looking American gentleman in his sixties asked me to direct him to the Ben Lomond footpath. It was about 3 p.m. He was dressed in a tweed jacket with collar and tie, and wearing very expensive street shoes. I explained that he had before him a rather messy, scrambling walk of about 11 kilometres or so down Loch Lomond side and that the ascent and descent of the Ben would take several hours. Even then, I had to work fairly hard to persuade him that the idea was, to say the least, ill-considered. His was only an extreme example of the way people are prepared to put themselves at risk through ignorance, and remember that even skilled and experienced people come to grief in the mountains. The good outdoor shops can supply you with a book about basic safety techniques. A good investment.

As we rose steadily towards the high point of our walk, the landscape became more grand, Malky waxed even more enthusiastic, and we were again among the plangent place names: Crow Craigies (crow rocks or cairns), Tom Buidhe (the yellow hill), the Knaps of Fafernie (knap – a mound or hill). We were also seeing higher tops now: Cairn Taggart and the White Mounth at over 1000 metres, and beyond, still with snow at nearly 1200 metres, the great bulk of Lochnagar. Yes, it is a mountain, not a loch.

The track negotiates the shoulder of Crow Craigies, but we made for the top at just over 900 metres. There would be many more hills before we were to reach the end of the Ardnamurchan peninsula, but we would never be higher again. Taking shelter in a hollow behind some rocks, Malky brought out the stove, and with some melted snow, we had a drum-up. Malky was under the illusion for some time that I had invited him along for his jolly nature, his charm and rapier wit, and for his outdoor skills. In fact I'd discovered that, like me, he loves his tea, and will drum up at every opportunity. Our effort to the top was further rewarded by a sighting of some ptarmigan, and by a

Above Loch Callater

combination of good luck and skill Barry managed to get them on film.

After a few miles of fairly straightforward hill walking, with deer and grouse scattering before us, we made the steep descent to Loch Callater; almost the roughest part of the track and very hard on the knees and thighs. There is a good Land Rover track on the far side of the loch, but we followed the much more attractive footpath along the east side. About halfway along, with Malky ahead, I disturbed a pair of sandpipers with their newly hatched chicks. They lay perfectly still, relying on their superb camouflage, and only the behaviour of the parent birds alerted me to their presence. A brief search and an even more brief photograph, and I left them to it. From the lodge at the end of Loch Callater, another good drum up point, a couple of kilometres of walking put us on to the road for Braemar.

A BLUFFER, A BEAUTY AND
A SHOW-OFF

S LUMPED BEHIND a couple of malt whiskies in Braemar, we agreed that the walk over Jock's Road had been the most stimulating part of the journey so far. We had stayed dry all day, if one ignores the stream of sweat down the backbone; visibility had been good and there was the feeling of physical well-being and satisfaction after a good, solid walk on high ground. One of the things Malky remembered especially was the sudden appearance of a grouse only a few metres ahead of us on the track and he was fascinated when it started flopping around like a rag doll. I was familiar with this behaviour, not only in grouse, but in many ground-nesting birds. It's the old 'Follow me, I'm wounded and easy prey' routine, designed to draw a predator away from eggs or young. Later, we were to be lucky enough to witness the same performance from a pair of golden plover, and once again I was struck by Malky's enthusiasm. As a hill man, he must have heard and probably seen the golden plover many times, but at close range and through the glasses, he was able to appreciate the spectacular beauty of this superb plover of the high tops. The plumage is black, white and gold, and the mournful, fluting call is one of the most evocative sounds in the hills.

The only one of the four types of Scottish grouse that we hadn't seen on the trip was the huge capercaillie. The name is from the Gaelic, Capull Coille, meaning 'horse of the woods'. The male is the size of a hefty turkey, and the species was re-introduced to Scotland from Scandinavia. Our other grouse are the red grouse, the black grouse, or black cock, and the ptarmigan.

The red grouse is found nowhere else but in Britain, the great bulk of the population being confined to Scotland, though the bird is found in England and Ireland in limited numbers. The red grouse is a handsome, tough-looking bird in russet brown plumage, with red wattles above the eye. It has powerful claws on whitish feathered legs, and as the cock birds are extremely aggressive in establishment and defence of breeding territory, they can and do inflict some damage. The rising and dipping flight seen early in the season is a mating display. Once the eggs have been laid, the well-camouflaged hens will sit until almost stood upon, then violently erupt under one's feet, a heart-stopping performance. The families stay together until late in the autumn and these are the ones usually mown down by the shooters. The ones taken by peregrine falcons or eagles are often birds which have been excluded from breeding territories. Anyone who has seen a red grouse rocketing across the heather will wonder how anything alive could catch it, but the peregrine easily outflies the grouse, whose usual escape tactic is a headlong plunge into the high heather.

The economy of many estates is often dependent on a good grouse season, and the moorland patchwork pattern caused by rotational burning is an important part of management. The young, tender shoots provide essential food, though the chicks also need protein in the form of insects, and the rank, high heather is required for nesting. Red grouse population densities fluctuate quite dramatically, a phenomenon which has been studied for many years. Despite extensive work by experts like Adam Watson of the Institute of Terrestrial Ecology, the reasons are not completely understood.

The ptarmigan is contemptuous of comfort, living on the high hills in conditions which even the tough-guy red grouse can't tolerate. A very beautiful bird, it looks quite different in summer and winter. The summer plumage is of a much paler greyish brown than that of the red grouse, with white wing feathers, and white feathered legs and feet. In the hard weather, the bird is camouflaged in snow white, with a little black on the tail, and a black stripe through the eye. These details tend to break up the outline of the bird, should it rest on a snowless patch. The cock birds are as aggressive as their red cousins and the females sit their eggs even more closely. As in the case of the little dotterel, another bird of the high tops, the ptarmigan probably has an instinctive reaction to the danger of rapid chilling of the eggs in such exposed places. A dotterel has been known to climb on to a human hand in order to continue brooding eggs which had been picked up.

The black grouse does not favour the open moors of the red, or the mountains of the ptarmigan, preferring to live in and along the edges of birch and coniferous woods. There is always open scrubby land nearby and this is where the famous leks take place. The lek is the breeding display, and often the chosen site has been used by generations of birds. The males gather in the early morning to pick up birds, and they do it in the usual way, by showing off. They are very showy indeed, with jet black plumage, a lyre-shaped tail (used to adorn many a Scottish bonnet), vivid red eye wattles, white hairy legs, and a patch of white under the tail. This last is much in evidence during the display to the females. The hen birds are, well, sort of dull.

The females are turned on by the flashiest and most aggressive cocks, mating takes place and that's the end of the relationship. The grey hens go off to lay eggs, rear chicks, and worry a lot. The males hang about until it's show-off time again . . .

BRAEMAR

I F ONE IS FORCED to make an overnight stop in a town, Braemar is as good as any, and much better than most. As soon as I arrived, I made it my business to contact Willie Meston, who is the Honorary Secretary of the Royal Highland Society which oversees the famous Braemar Royal Highland Games. Willie is a handsome, robust figure, who looks the way people should in the kilt, but seldom do. He is also pretty knowledgeable about the Braemar games. The games are probably the best known in Scotland, and almost certainly the most ancient, going back to the time of King Malcolm Canmore in the eleventh century.

Willie Meston

Legend has it that Malcolm called the clans together for a test of speed, strength, endurance and courage, so that he could select the best as soldiers. No one seems to have had the common sense to turn in a bad performance. When the King offered a purse of gold and a sword to the first man to get to the top and back of Craig Choinich (the wooded crag), competition was keen. Two Macgregor brothers were much fancied to win but were foiled by a younger brother who, despite a late start, raced ahead. One of the older Macgregors, true to his perfidious name, clutched at the speedy youngster's kilt, but to no avail. The young man broke free to win the race, the purse, the sword and the jolly life of a soldier in the eleventh century.

The games became official in 1800, when veterans of the Napoleonic War met to test their manhood by lifting the Clach Cuid Fir, a huge stone which, in some cases, probably ruined it. Those who escaped a hernia went on to have a go at dancing, piping and foot races. The Braemar Royal Highland Games became royal when Queen Victoria and Prince Albert attended in 1848, and they have remained royal ever since.

Braemar is a particularly Scottish-looking place, and has been a popular tourist centre since Queen Victoria took a fancy to Deeside, and established the area as a haunt of the royals. Where there are royals there are tourists, but Braemar has more to offer than its royal connections, standing as it does at the junction of the Clunie Water and the River Dee, and circled by some of Scotland's most impressive mountains. The town's historic connections are endless. Robert Louis Stevenson spent the summer of 1881 in a cottage in Braemar, and it was there that he wrote *Treasure Island*. Braemar Castle, which is still occupied, was built by the Earl of Mar, and it was here, on the Braes of Mar, that the 'Noble Mar' raised the Jacobite standard for King James VIII in August 1715. Thirty years later, Bonnie Prince Charlie was to make the final and catastrophic attempt to restore the 400-year-old dynasty of the Stuarts. Ironically, the castle was used for many years as a barracks to keep an eye on any potentially troublesome Jacobites, in the aftermath of the 1745 rising.

Our route from Braemar to White Bridge and on to Glen Tilt would take us past three well-known local landmarks: Mar Lodge, Inverey, and the Linn of Dee. Mar Lodge stands on the north side of the river. Queen Victoria laid the first stone in 1896, and the house

By White Bridge

was eventually occupied by her granddaughter, Princess Louise, the Duchess of Fife. About 3 kilometres along the river is another of the area's much-vaunted tourist attractions: the Linn of Dee. At this point, the river rushes through a deep cleft in the rocks, creating a marvellous spectacle, especially when there is a spate or late in the summer, when the salmon make their spectacular leaps up the torrent. Between Mar Lodge and the Linn, the village of Inverey is divided by the Ey bridge into Little Inverey and Muckle Inverey. Inverey gave us one of our great Scottish ballads.

INVEREY

Doon Deeside cam Inverey a-whistling and playing
And he was at Brackley's yetts ere the day was dawing.
'O are ye there Brackley, and are ye within?
There's sherp swords are at your yetts
Will mak your bluid spin.

'Then rise up my Baron and turn back your kye*,
For the lads frae Drumwharron are driving them bye.'
'O how can I rise up and how can I gang?
For whaur I hae ae man, I'm sure they hae ten.

'But rise up Betsy Gordon and gie me my gun,
And 'though I gang oot love, sure I'll never return.
Come kiss me my Betsy, nor think I'm tae blame,
But against three and thirty, wae's me, whit is ane?'

When Brackley was mounted and rade on his horse,
A bonnier baron ne'er rade ower a course.
Two gallanter Gordons did never sword draw,
But against three and thirty, wae's me, whit is twa?

Wi' their dirks and their swords they did him surroond,
And they've killed Bonnie Brackley wi' mony's the wound.
Frae the heid o' the Dee tae the banks o' the Spey,
The Gordons shall mourn him, and ban Inverey.

'O cam ye by Brackley or cam ye by here,
Or saw ye his guid lady a-tearing her hair?'
'O I cam by Brackley and I cam by here,
And I saw his guid lady, she was making guid cheer.

'She was ranting and dancing and singing for joy,
She vowed that very nicht she wad feast Inverey.
She lauched wi' him, danced wi' him, welcomed him in;
She was kind til the villain wha had slain her guid man.'

Through hedges and ditches ye canna be sure,
Through the woods o' Drumwharron ye maun slap in an hoor.
Then up spake the babe on his nannie's knee:
'It's afore I'm a man avenged I'll be.'

Collated and condensed by Robin Hall from
Last Leaves of Traditional Ballads

---

* *kye* = cattle

GLEN TILT, AN OLD ENEMY
AND A HARDY OLD BIRD

ROM THE LINN OF DEE, five kilometres of easy walking took us to the White Bridge, with two of the big Cairngorm mountains: Beinn a Bhuird at 1196 metres, and Ben Avon at 1171 metres well behind us. The last view I had had of Ben Avon was from the summit, where I had finished my walk of the Speyside Way in the company of stalker John McDonald. I remembered that we had just managed to get our final shot and closing link of the whole television series, before being chased off the mountain by a sudden flurry of snow.

At Dubrach, on the way to the bridge, lie the ruins of the redcoat garrison established after the 1745 rising. Here, too, lived a man called Peter Grant, who was one of a small group involved in both the 1715 and 1745 Jacobite uprisings. He fought with Bonnie Prince Charlie, and was a staunch Jacobite to the end. He was taken to meet King George IV in Edinburgh, and when the King shook his hand, saying, 'You are my oldest friend,' the old boy replied, 'Na, na, your majesty, I am your oldest enemy'. King George appeared to be charmed rather than offended, and gave Grant a pension of £52 per year for life. The generosity of the gesture has to be balanced against the fact that Peter was already 108 years old, but the pension began immediately and was paid weekly. At Peter Grant's graveside, the pipers played him off with 'Wha Wadna Fecht for Chairlie'.

At the White Bridge, Malky's trusty stove made its appearance again, and the tea was soon brewing while we had a look at the map. There are two well-known routes which begin here. One goes north up Glen Dee and through the famous Lairig Ghru between some very big mountains indeed: Cairn Toul and Braeriach both at over 1200 metres and the biggest of them all, Beinn Macduibh at 1309 metres. Our route would take us south-west along Glen Tilt and on to Blair Atholl; quite hard going for nearly 39 kilometres, but we had decided to camp along the way.

Before leaving White Bridge I had a few words with a group of very jolly young girls who were on the Duke of Edinburgh's Award Scheme. I met some of them a couple of months later when I was one of several people chosen to assist the Duke in the presentation of the awards at Holyrood Palace. They were rather taken aback to see me

Bedford Bridge

tarted up in full highland dress, and I was equally confused to see those sun-browned raggedy hikers in long posh goonies and floppy hats.

A little way on from the White Bridge we were faced with the crossing of the Geldie Burn. Local stalker Stuart Cumming told us that he had seen the burn enormously swollen by rain coming down from the high ground, and the huge flat surrounding area totally inundated. We were lucky, for although there weren't quite enough exposed stepping stones, the water was low enough for us to wade. Malky replaced his boots with a pair of trainers but I simply removed my socks, put the boots back on, waded over thigh deep, and emptied my boots on the other side. On a breezy, sunny day, they were soon dry.

We had 3 or 4 kilometres of flat, easy walking now, past the ruin of the old Bynack Lodge, before we entered Glen Tilt. The path, which the Duke of Atholl tried to close in the last century, now took on a quite different character. Wide enough for only one person, it undulated, sometimes quite steeply, along the shoulder of a 45° slope. Beneath, to our left, were the torrents, the falls, the deep, mysterious pools and fantastic rock formations of the River Tilt. The steep, narrow track winding on mile after mile demanded concentration, but we did indulge in some idle chat. Malky: 'Mind you, she must have been a pretty hardy old bird.' Me: 'Who?' M: 'Old Queen Vicky.' Me: 'What do you mean?' M: 'Well, she did the trip from Balmoral to Blair Atholl in 1861, didn't she?' Me: 'Yes, Malky, but I don't think she legged it for 39 kilometres along a sheep track.' M: 'Aye; right.'

Twenty-two kilometres from the Linn of Dee, the Tarf Water rushes spectacularly through a deep gorge in a series of falls, cascades and deep pools, to join the River Tilt, and it was here that we made a brief stop. Malky had a quick dip in one of the icy-cold pools, while I drummed up. The Tarf is crossed here by the elegant timber and wrought-iron Bedford Memorial Bridge. A metal plaque fixed to the structure carries the message: 'This bridge was erected in 1886 with funds contributed by his friends and others, and by the Scottish Rights of Way Society Ltd, to commemorate the death of Francis John Bedford, aged eighteen, who was drowned near here on 25 August 1879.'

TAME STAGS AND A 2-INCH TELLY

WE STILL HAD 22 kilometres to go to Blair Atholl, but the glen and river were so beautiful and inviting that we decided to camp near Forest Lodge. The one interest I found difficult to share with Malky was his devotion to footba''. The World Cup was in full swing as we made our coast-to-coast journey, turning this extrovert and easy-going man into a brooding neurotic when things weren't going so well for 'the boys', which was most of the time. With the occasional upturn in the fortunes of the Scottish team, Malky became radiantly joyful, and found it difficult

to comprehend my lack of interest. In fact, we had a mildly entertaining running gag on the go: Malky playing up his fanaticism (but not much) and me pretending to be totally indifferent, rather than almost totally indifferent as to whether 'the boys done good'.

Malky carried one of those miniaturised television receivers everywhere, and monitored the progress of the cup competition whenever possible. Sweden played Scotland on the evening that we camped in Glen Tilt, and there was a bizarre scene, as two grubby, midgie-bitten people crouched by a wood fire at dusk, to watch a football match being transmitted live from Genoa to a 2-inch TV screen in a Scottish glen miles from anywhere. The score was 2–1, and we won. Or Sweden did. I can't remember.

At Forest Lodge, we met keeper Ron MacGregor, a quiet and likeable man with a lifetime of outdoor experience, and many a tale from his observations of wildlife. He told me that he'd seen foxes leaping a metre or more straight up to snatch a grouse from the air, and of people keeping tame stags. They apparently take quite easily to humans, but can become dangerous as they get older, particularly at the time of the rut. Ron told me that the Duke of Fife for a long time refused to get rid of one which terrorised his workers on the Mar estate. There were many complaints, but to no avail, and this went on until the stag made the serious error of turning on the Duke himself, who suffered the indignity of having to leap through a window to escape the animal. End of stag, end of problem.

Interesting company though he was, Ron was seriously upstaged by Mrs MacGregor, who appeared unannounced with a huge pot of tea and a superb selection of her home baking. Thus fortified, we set off for Blair Atholl.

BLAIR ATHOLL

B LAIR ATHOLL is a very attractive village dominated by the castle around which it has grown. The ancestral home of the earls and dukes of Atholl, the castle is Scottish baronial but without the heavy, forbidding appearance associated with that style. The brilliant white surfaces and oddly placed turrets give the building a fairy-tale quality which is very appealing indeed.

The oldest part of the structure, known as Comyn's Tower, was built by John Comyn of Badenoch in 1269, and has undergone many alterations and additions at the hands of successive owners. Edward III called by in 1336, and when Mary, Queen of Scots, arrived in 1564, a grand hunt was arranged in the Forest of Atholl, in which 360 deer and five wolves were killed. The castle was occupied by Montrose in 1644, and Cromwell gave it his usual treatment in 1653. No sooner had the builders cleaned up the mess than it was occupied by Graham of Claverhouse in 1689.

The first Duke of Atholl was granted that title by Queen Anne and, though a staunch royalist, he protested very strongly about the government-inspired massacre in Glencoe. He later resisted the union with England in 1707, arguing for better terms. Whether for Scotland or himself may be in doubt; many noble Scottish palms were crossed with silver in that auspicious conjunction.

The family was divided in its loyalties, and the first Duke found himself with one son, James, sharing his views, while his other three sons William, Marquis of Tullibardine, Lord Charles and Lord

George supported the Jacobites. Bonnie Prince Charlie stayed twice in the castle: once in his eager march south, and again on the weary trudge to annihilation at Culloden. In 1746, Lord George Murray, who had become one of the Prince's more able officers, found himself laying siege to what had been his own home.

I was disappointed not to meet the Duke on this occasion, as he was in France, but I had interviewed him at one of the annual Grant's Whisky piping championships, which are held in the great ballroom. This wonderful flag-draped room with its superb timber-beamed roof has portraits of the various Dukes of Atholl and a very famous one by Sir Henry Raeburn of Neil Gow, who was fiddler to the second, third and fourth Dukes. The present Duke told me that at one time a horse and cart travelled up and down from the village, all day, every day, with the coal required to heat the huge building. I also learned that the fine policies and woodlands were established by an ancestor known as the Planting Duke. He started in the 1760s, and by 1830, when the fourth Duke died, about 14 million trees had been planted.

We spent the greater part of the day at Blair Castle, as producer Dennis Dick had decided to film the ceremonial firing of the cannon. This is quite a spectacle, and fascinating to visitors from abroad, who are somehow always astounded when the thing actually goes off. There are always oohs and aahs and hysterical giggles of fright, but everyone enjoys it enormously. The exercise is carried out by the men of the Atholl Highlanders. On this occasion the event was in the command of Regimental Sergeant Major Peter Kemp, and was followed by a tune from piper Eddie Clark. The tenth Duke of Atholl is the only person in Britain with a dispensation to maintain a private army, and on 18 April 1990 he kindly joined me on my daily radio programme, *Macgregor's Gathering*, to tell me about it.

The Atholl Highlanders were first raised to fight for King George III in the American War of Independence, but were good enough sports to return for the 200th anniversary celebrations of the signing of the American constitution. In 1783, they were ordered to the East Indies. They were not such good sports about this, and mutinied. Amazingly, they got away with it, and the regiment was disbanded soon after. Much later, when Sir Walter Scott staged his famous Scottish pantomime for King George IV, the Duke asked for 100 men to parade in Edinburgh, but they were, in fact, inspected at Dunkeld.

The Atholl Men

The army was, by this time, a part-time affair, but the presentation of colours by Queen Victoria in 1842 gave it the right to bear arms. Between 1914 and 1966, when they were reinstated, there had been only four parades by the Atholl Highlanders. Thanks to the enthusiasm and commitment of Iain, the present Duke, and of the men themselves, Scotland's only private army now presents a familiar, colourful spectacle, not only in Scotland but also overseas. Four members of the Highlanders who were presented to Crown Prince Akihito of Japan, now have the rare distinction of holding the Order of the Rising Sun. They are Sergeant-Major McArthur, Pipe-Major Stewart, Pipe-Corporal Irvine and Private Sinclair.

A GRIM LADY, A BATTLE AND A DANGEROUS CROSSING

AS WE LEFT BLAIR ATHOLL, we passed an old water mill where I had once recorded an entire radio programme. The interviews were beautifully enhanced by the sounds of a working mill: the clacking and sloshing of the great wheel, the creaking of timbers and the grinding of the stones. My only regret was that I was unable to record the wonderful smells. The mill is now in the charge of Mrs Ridley, whose husband took the building on as a ruin and restored it to life. It is now run by the head miller, Stephen Page from Blairgowrie, and assistant miller Robert Ross from Blair Atholl.

Having walked along the river bank behind some lovely old single-

The Mill, Blair Atholl

storey estate cottages, we crossed the river and stopped in a woody lane, where I did some explaining to camera of where I was and what my next move would be. Halfway through this process, I was interrupted by a rather grim-faced lady who emerged quite easily from her garden to announce, in a rather posh English voice, that she took great exception to *not* being able to emerge easily from her garden. As we were filming several yards up the lane, I was rather puzzled by this. Malky wasn't puzzled; Malky was fizzing. He has a bee in his bonnet, for some reason or other, about the fact that every other post office, bed and breakfast establishment, old manse, hotel, craft shop and sporting estate appears to be in the hands of incomers. He can be a very unreasonable wee Scot sometimes.

Before the disgruntled property owner had brought proceedings to a halt, I had been explaining that there is a choice of routes from this point over to Loch Tummel. Some people even make a detour to the scene of the Battle of Killiecrankie. This famous stramash in the Pass of Killiecrankie was led on one hand by John Graham of Claverhouse, Viscount Dundee, known as Bonnie Dundee; and on the other by General Mackay, a fully paid-up Presbyterian and fervent supporter of King William III.

The song, *Bonnie Dundee*, reflects Claverhouse's defiant gesture against the acceptance of King William, and his resolve to raise an army against him. 'The Braes o' Killiecrankie' purports to tell the story of the battle itself, in which Bonnie Dundee was mortally wounded in his hour of triumph. He was carried from the field to the House of Orrat nearby, where he wrote a letter to the Stuart King James, telling of his victory. He died before morning.

We now had to face the most hazardous part of our jouney so far – the crossing of the A9 road. Conditions were dreadful. The rain battering down was met about a metre or so off the ground by the spray flying up, and the bumper-to-bumper juggernauts threw up bow waves at supersonic speeds. Sheer raw courage and the footwork of a couple of flyweight boxers took us to the other side, drookit and diesel-stained, but alive. A couple of kilometres over the hill through a dripping wood brought us to Fincastle and on to Loch Tummel.

LOCH TUMMEL, FENCIBLES AND A FAIRY HILL

L OCH TUMMEL IS FAMOUS for two reasons: Queen's View and 'The Road to the Isles', a popular Scottish song in which it is mentioned. Queen's View is on a towering promontory over the narrow, eastern end of the loch, and commands a splendid panorama which takes in much of the surrounding countryside, including the massive bulk of Schiehallion at the far end of the waters. It was raining when we arrived so I had to console myself with memories of my youth hostelling days, when I had surveyed the scene in brilliant sunlight.

THE ROAD TO THE ISLES

A far crooning is pulling me away,
As tak I wi' my cromak to the road;
The far Coolins are putting love on me,
As step I wi' the sunlight for my load.

CHORUS
    Sure by Tummel and Loch Rannoch and Lochaber I will go,
    By heather tracks wi' heaven in their wiles;
    If it's thinking in your inner heart the braggart's in my step,
    You've never smelled the tangle o' the Isles.

It's by Shiel water the track is to the west,
By Aillort and by Morar to the sea;
The cool cresses I am thinking o' for pluck,
And bracken for a wink on mother knee.

CHORUS

O' the blue islands are pulling me away,
Their laughter puts the leap upon the lame.
The blue islands from the skerries to the Lews,
Wi' heather honey taste upon each name.

CHORUS

Most people assume, as I did, that Queen's View is so named from the visit of Queen Victoria, but it appears that Mary Queen of Scots pre-empted Victoria. Legend has it that she was so impressed that she had her harper compose an air in praise of the beauty of the scene. The Forestry Commission has a cleverly thought-out visitors' centre close by, where one can learn something of the area's wildlife, forestry work, history, and local forest walks.

A very famous Macgregor lived here. When the horrendously repressive proscriptions against Clan Gregor were at long last repealed by King George, the appreciative 'Children of the Mist' raised their own regiment, the Clan Alpine Fencibles. The Fencibles were a Scotland-wide home guard, a sort of eighteenth-century Dad's Army raised to resist the threatened invasion by Napoleon. There had been much sympathy in Scotland for the ideals of the French Revolution, but when the little corporal turned his eye on our shores, many of his erstwhile supporters changed their stance. Even Robert Burns, who was very much in tune with the concepts of *Liberté*, *Egalité*, *Fraternité*, became a volunteer in the Dumfries Fencibles.

When John Macgregor, who came from a little village near Kinloch Rannoch, enlisted in the Fencibles, he was joined by his son Duncan, who became a commissioned officer, and ensign, at the age of twelve. He kept up the pace, subsequently becoming a general, after serving in campaigns in various parts of the world, and lived until he was ninety-four.

Schiehallion,
Loch Tummel

Schiehallion is a splendidly isolated cone-shaped mountain lying to the south of the gap between Loch Tummel and Loch Rannoch. It's a big one too, at 1081 metres, and has been endlessly painted, photographed, written and sung about. In 1774, Maskelyne, the Astronomer Royal, made use of Schiehallion in experiments to calculate the attraction of the mass of mountains, and the mathematician Charles Hutton later deduced the density of the earth from Maskelyne's work. Schiehallion is known as the Fairy Hill of Caledon.

MORNING LIGHT AND
BODY MEMORIES

A T LOCH TUMMEL, we had arranged to stay at Dalcroy Farm, a beautiful and peaceful place backing on to the loch shore. The other, more recent name of the farm is Morning Light, and it is run by Clive and Peggy Malcouronne with the help of a dedicated staff: Veronica, George and Helen, Brenda, Linda, and George and Sandy. Morning Light operates as a straightforward guest house offering peace and quiet in lovely tranquil surroundings, but Clive Malcouronne has established something there which is very special. He offers therapy to people who have been victims of child abuse, and with the aid of a variety of techniques, including hypnosis, tackles emotional, psychological, and even physical problems.

53

Clive is a quietly spoken man with a definite air of gentleness and kindliness about him. He is an admirer and follower of Dr Woolger, whose book on past-life experiences and regressive therapy Clive claims to be the most perceptive treatise on this mysterious and fascinating subject. As a devotee of Dr Woolger's theories, Clive has spent many years investigating past-life therapy and the concept of body memory. In simple terms, as explained to me by Clive, the work is rooted in the belief that many of our deep-seated psychological problems, and even some physical ones, derive from trauma in past life; and the therapist's technique is to take the subject back to that previous existence and isolate the problem.

For most people, these ideas defy all logic and received wisdom, but there is absolutely no doubt of Clive Malcouronne's deep sincerity and his conviction that he can be, and has been, of help to a great many people. Dr Woolger has documented over 3000 cases, some of them very dramatic indeed. The subject is vast, subtle, and beyond my comprehension. It is certainly beyond the scope of this book, but Clive sent me a tape of one of his cases which makes riveting listening.

A young man introduces himself as Richard Harlow and, under Clive's hypnosis, he goes back through various stages of his life, with richly detailed memories, and eventually to his own birth. Through this part of the tape, his voice, breathing and style of delivery change constantly, until he eventually arrives at the persona of one Ralph Smythe, a nineteen-year-old airman in the First World War. Here, the voice and personality are quite different. He talks knowledgeably, in the slang of the time, of his colleagues and superior officers; about the inadequacy of the British aircraft; and of the ever-present terror of becoming a flamer: to be trapped in a burning plane. Richard Harlow's/Ralph Smythe's account of his aircraft being destroyed on a photographic reconnaissance, and the long fall to earth with his Scottish cameraman is graphic and harrowing. If this is acting, it is acting of a very high calibre indeed, reducing a friend of mine to tears of compassion on hearing it.

Clive Malcouronne's researches showed that a nineteen-year-old First World War airman called Ralph Smythe did die as described. I am totally unqualified to endorse or criticise this aspect of the work being done at Morning Light. What I do know is that Clive and Peggy and their staff are devoted to helping people.

KUCHEN MIT SAHNE AND CAMUSERICHT

W E WERE REALLY on the famous Road to the Isles now, and the walk along Loch Tummel and the river Tummel to Loch Rannoch was favoured by brilliant sunshine and a few refreshing showers. By the side of the road, I pointed out to Malky the agitated behaviour of a little willow warbler with a beak fringed with insects, a sure sign of a nearby nest. By simply staying still for a few minutes we reassured the bird sufficiently for it to fly down to the verge and get on with the business of feeding five rapidly growing and insatiable chicks. I was then able to show Malky the cleverly concealed and finely constructed little domed nest with its side entrance.

Stopping only long enough to take some photographs of the sunlit cone of Schiehallion, we made our way along Loch Rannoch, until arrested by a roadside sign which advertised *Kuchen mit Sahne*. This was at Talladh-a-Bheithe and, almost in unison, Malky and I exclaimed, 'Well, it makes a change from the English', and off we went up the drive to see what it was all about. *Kuchen mit Sahne* means cakes with cream and what it was all about was mouth-watering, eye-bulging, waist-distending, thrombosis-inducing, wonderful German cakes and home baking, made and served by a delightful, friendly German lady called Gertrud. Needless to say, we stayed longer and

With Gertrud at
Talladh-a-Bheithe

ate more than was sensible, but eventually got our bloated bodies and heavy legs back on the Road to the Isles, with fond memories of Gertrud and Talladh-a-Bheithe. Talladh-a-Bheithe used to be Tal-a-bheithe, which meant the rock among the birches. The present name, Talladh, means a hall.

I had been told about a place called Camusericht Lodge, which lay towards the western end of Loch Rannoch, and we made that our next stop. Camusericht is a large, traditional Scottish lodge, which is run by Anita Irvin and her husband. Mr Irvin has business interests elsewhere, but looks after the long-term policy decisions, while Anita has responsibility for day-to-day management. This she appears to do with efficiency and considerable charm and we found her a very personable hostess. With the lodge goes a 12 500-acre sporting estate, offering stag, grouse, blackcock and ptarmigan. The estate is mainly deer forest, and Anita told me that as well as the usual stag shooting, she has no problem in filling the house with winter guests who are prepared to face the hardships of stalking hinds in rigorous conditions for the compensations of fairly luxurious conditions afterwards. Anita Irvin chooses to run the lodge not as an hotel, but as a very comfortable home, with house guests. The food is excellent and the atmosphere is one of peace and relaxation. The surroundings are very interesting, with antiques, paintings, and stuffed birds and fish everywhere. We relished Camusericht as a contrast to our next intended stopping place, which was to be Loch Ossian Youth Hostel.

'A DESERT WILD AND WASTED'
AND A ROUGH WOOING

THE NAME CAMUSERICHT can mean the bend in the River Ericht, or it can mean the bay, and it was on the little pier in a bay close to the lodge that producer Dennis Dick and I considered our next move, with Malky, camera and sound men Barry and Bob, and Iain Murray, who probably knew the next stretch of the walk better than any of us. The Rannoch Moor is a wilderness of more than 125 square kilometres, and not to be taken lightly. The terrain is low hills, and very broken and featureless ground dotted and pitted with countless lochans and peat hags. In very wet or misty conditions it can be dangerous, and in winter, potentially deadly. We were about

Rannoch Moor

to cross in circumstances which were as good as one was likely to find. There had been no really heavy rainfall for some time, so that the going would be reasonably dry most of the time, and the weather was quite sunny and breezy. After discussing the alternatives, which were Land Rover or train, we decided that we should leg it, and that Barry and Bob should manhandle the camera and tape recorder as far as Loch Ossian, where we should think again.

We made our way from Loch Rannoch by the old Rannoch Barracks on the south side of the River Gaur (the winter stream) and past the power station where the river enters Loch Eigheach. At the point where we left the road for the track which would take us across to Loch Ossian and on to Glen Nevis, there is a sign which informed us officially that this was indeed the 'Road to the Isles'. It was here that we met stalker Colin Robertson, who informed me that he had proposed to his wife on the summit of a neighbouring steep hill. 'She didn't have much choice,' Colin told me. 'I said that I'd push her off if she refused.' This sophisticated approach apparently paid off, for Colin went on to assure me that he is still happily married.

The lines which describe the moor as 'A desert wild and wasted' describe one of many impressions of this awesome place and in his novel *The New Road*, Neil Munro has one of his characters observing that the great moor of Rannoch was 'The oddest thing, the eeriest in nature that he had ever seen'. Many people will remember the hunt on the moor for Alan Breck and David Balfour in Robert Louis Stevenson's *Kidnapped*. It has been remarked that had Stevenson really known the moor, he would have seen the improbability of dragoons and horses being able to negotiate such terrain. Sir Walter Scott's words, 'A land of desolation and grey darkness', seemed quite inappropriate as we broke out the stove and billy can at the ruins of the old Corrour Lodge. The whole vast expanse, ringed by mountains, was bathed in sunlight and dappled by the shadows of racing clouds. The Lodge of Corrour was used as a sanatorium at one time and if fresh air has the restorative properties which were assumed at the time then I imagine that the patients here would have been up and running in no time at all. From the vantage point of the lodge on the slope, we could look ahead to the distant gleam of snow on Ben Nevis and, to the south-west, the bulk of the Buachaille Etive Mór, in Glencoe, beyond the waters of the Blackwater Reservoir.

The reservoir was created by the construction of a dam which joined three lochs to create a stretch of water 13 kilometres long. The dam itself is over 300 metres long, and nearly 30 metres high. It was built by itinerant navvies early this century, to provide power for the aluminium smelting works at Kinlochleven, and a by-product was electric lighting for the town.

A FLOATING RAILWAY AND
A STRANGE JOURNEY

THE TRACK, SUCH AS IT WAS, led almost due north for a little way before swinging north-west towards the old ruined lodge of Corrour. The way rose steadily, with many an up and down, along the lower shoulder of Sron Leachd a' Chaorainn, and we were able to watch a train snaking across below us, its size and speed diminished by the vast scale of the moor.

Running a railway across this forbidding waste was a task to challenge even the most dynamic engineers and entrepreneurs of the Victorian era. The peat is several metres deep in some places, and in others the railway has to cross bogs which never dry out. This prob-

Ben Nevis from
Corrour Lodge

lem was resolved by floating the lines on a layer of ash, brushwood, heather roots and stones, and it's said that on some parts of the line one can see the rails undulating under the weight of the train. In 1889, seven people who were surveying the route became lost in the mist, and it was sheer good fortune that led one of them to a shepherd's house. A search was mounted and the others were found. That night a blizzard blew up which would certainly have killed them had they remained on the moor. The enterprise went ahead, and the West Highland Line is now recognised as one of the most dramatic scenic railway journeys in the world.

It was an extremely dramatic, if not very scenic, journey for the guard of one particular steam train known on the West Highland Line as 'The Ghost'. Near Corrour station, at the head of the long incline from Rannoch station, the coupling snapped between the guard's van and the rest of the train. The guard was blissfully asleep as his van began to gently roll back in the direction of Rannoch, watched by the helpless signalman at Corrour. By the time it came into view at

Rannoch, the van had picked up a lot of speed and was obviously a runaway. The rules dictated that it should be derailed, but the Rannoch signalman knew that this would almost certainly result in the death of the guard. The station at Gorton was informed and again the signalman took no action, praying that it would manage all the bends before Bridge of Orchy station.

Three kilometres past Bridge of Orchy station, the van came to a standstill and when a puffing signalman arrived, he found the guard still soundly asleep. He was wakened with some difficulty, and could not believe that he had made a round trip of 80 kilometres, and was back where he had been two hours before, and alive.

LOCH OSSIAN: A MEMORIAL
AND A LATIN LOVER

ON LEAVING THE evocative ruins of Corrour Lodge with its resonances of past lives, we were soon looking down on the wooded shores of Loch Ossian. The path divides here for the shooting lodge at the eastern end of the loch, and the youth hostel at the other. As we commenced the descent we came upon a flat rock with a metal plaque attached. It read:

> *In memory of Peter J. Trowell*
> *Born Sept. 1949. Died March 1979 at Loch Ossian.*
> *I have a song, a friend and a glass,*
> *Gaily along life's road I pass,*
> *Joyous and free out of doors for me,*
> *Over the hills in the morning.*

Not, perhaps, the best poetry ever penned, but obviously a sincere and heartfelt tribute. We were to hear more of Peter Trowell at Loch Ossian hostel.

Even by Scottish standards, Loch Ossian is a pretty remote hostel. Most people walk in from the Loch Rannoch end, or over from Glen Nevis, but it is possible to cheat, as we almost did, and take the train to Corrour station, leaving only a short walk to the end of the loch. Loch Ossian is the way I remember hostels when I was a lad. It's a wooden building, though with a good, slated roof. There are two small

Loch Ossian

dormitories and a common room which is dominated by a big iron stove, with a pipe chimney going up through the roof. In the evenings, and especially in rough weather in this wild place, the atmosphere is wonderfully snug. The stove is nearly red hot, and the huge kettle is bouncing and bubbling away to supply the endless cups of tea which seems to be the life blood of most hostellers. The chat is all of climbs, walks, adventures and misadventures in the hills, and, with the proximity of the loch, of fishing and fishermen.

On the night we stayed there, most of the hostellers were veterans, some of them quite elderly, but still very much enjoying the outdoor life. Malky, surrounded by all these interesting faces, was drawing frantically. One young Italian was making quite an impression on two even younger German girls, and obviously saw himself as the definitive latin lover. He was a good-looking lad for sure, with the obligatory dark eyes and lots of carefully wild curly hair, and was taken aback by Malky's deadly accurate caricature, which showed the nose a shade longer than average, and the ears just a wee bit flappy. 'Who's-a-that?' he asked, failing to realise that it was exactly him. However, as Malky predicted, the drawing was carefully packed away to be shown off back home in Italy.

(*Above*)
Loch Ossian Hostel, Tom Rigg
and Malky

(*Right*)
A serious warning

The gents' ablutions at the hostel consist of a bench with some buckets and basins. A lot of things are done in buckets and basins at Loch Ossian. On the narrow strip between the back of the hostel and the loch shore, there is a facility normally seen only in cowboy films: a small wooden shed containing, yes, another bucket. Users are warned of potential embarrassment by a printed sign which says, 'Please bolt the door or it blows away.' Another helpful message informs the more pressured hosteller, 'You may pee on the grass if you wish.'

The warden here is Tom Rigg, a long-time outdoor man who takes an almost obsessive interest in the place. He has gradually tamed several stags by enticing them down from the hills with delicacies such as potatoes, turnips and, most toothsome of all, apples. There is something very comforting, on turning in for the night, to look out into the gloaming and see three fully grown stags settling down on the loch shore only yards from the hostel window. Tom, who has been at Loch Ossian for some years, knows the surrounding area very well, and has a wealth of stories of past walkers and climbers. The saddest is that of Peter Trowell, whose memorial plaque we had seen on the hill.

Peter was an old friend who had come to stay at the hostel, but the visit was unannounced and Tom Rigg was away. Furthermore, Peter had informed no one of his plans, and several days passed before anyone noticed that he was missing. Only then were enquiries made, and it was established that he had been seen alighting from the train at Corrour station. The alarm was raised and a huge search was made of the surrounding hills, but to no avail.

It was Tom Rigg who persuaded the searchers that they were looking in the wrong place. Tom was convinced that his friend was somewhere in the waters of the loch. Dragging was out of the question, but divers were sent under the ice. They emerged quite convinced that there was no body in Loch Ossian. Tom was equally sure, having observed a hole in the ice which had re-frozen over. His theory of the cause of Peter's death was proved tragically correct. The young man had slipped on the frozen timbers of the old pier and had fallen several feet to crash head first through the ice. The body surfaced some weeks later, rucksack still attached.

MORGAN THE POST, THE FOMORIANS AND THE CLOVEN HOOF

THE SECTION OF RANNOCH MOOR from Loch Ossian is quite a demanding walk of 25 or so very rough kilometres, with a few more down to Glen Nevis. The weather was uncertain, and it was decided that Barry and Bob would see us off, then go round by road with the gear and come as far up Glen Nevis as they could manage, to film our arrival. We had an early breakfast, fed a few more potatoes to the stags, said our goodbyes to Tom Rigg, and were about to step out, when Mrs Morgan the post arrived. This was an old friend whom I had interviewed when she and her husband ran the now unmanned Corrour station. Mrs Morgan is a plump, jolly person who describes herself as one of the area's endangered species. She

certainly looked like an exotic species, as she roared up to the hostel door on a balloon-tyred mountain bike, attired in crash-helmet and violently coloured spacesuit. The suit is warm and deliberately very visible, for when the tracks are impassable, Mrs Morgan simply takes to the hills to deliver her mail. Halfway to Glen Nevis I was wishing she'd show up with space for a pillion passenger.

After about 8 kilometres of steady plodding, our path took us along the shore of Loch Treig. This is where the railway line abandons the open moor to run north along the loch before curling west again to Fort William. Loch Treig and the Blackwater Reservoir are the biggest stretches of water on the moor, the only other loch of any size being Loch Laidon. There are two more, called Loch Eilde Mór (big) and Loch Eilde Beag (small), but the whole vast area glitters in bright weather with a myriad little lochans, peat hags, dubs and rivulets. Rannoch Moor was scraped, gouged and flattened thousands of years ago by glaciation which deposited millions of stones over the surface, some of them of colossal size and strange conformation. The Gaels quite naturally explained this giant debris as the work of giants.

The Fomorians were a pair of outsize bully boys who apparently gave the locals many a headache, until taken to task by a young man who favoured brain against brawn. He arranged a meeting with the

(*Page 64*)
Morgan the Post

(*Left*)
Robbie Campbell

giants, and after many flattering observations on their great size and strength, set up a stone-throwing competition between the naturally quarrelsome and competitive pair. The stones became greater and heavier as the competition went on, until the giants were almost exhausted. The loser, piqued at being out-thrown, rather naughtily flattened his rival with the final chuckie before collapsing and dying of exhaustion. The local people were very glad to be rid of the tiresome towering-twosome, but never did get round to tidying up the stones.

Stories like this abound in the region, as indeed they do all over the Highlands, and not long ago I interviewed a man on my radio programme who had gathered the best of them together in a book called *Tales of Rannoch*. The author's name is A. D. Cunningham, and he has come up with irresistible titles like 'The Egg Faced Man', 'The Black Walker of the Ford', 'The Death Cart at Learan' and 'The Stone of the Heads'. Mr Cunningham tells one wonderful story of a stranger who appears from nowhere and joins in a card game in a remote house near Loch Treig. One of the players drops his cards, and in bending to retrieve them, sees that the stranger has the cloven, iron-shod hooves of the devil . . . There are modern stories too of inexplicable happenings on the moor, such as rescuers being led unaccountably to lost victims. One can believe almost anything of this strange place.

A lot of determined trudging, one rather difficult river crossing and a period of floundering through some seemingly endless peat bog brought us, muddy, drenched and weary, but triumphant, to the head of Glen Nevis.

Robbie Campbell is a young shepherd who herds in the glen. A big, blond, robust lad, he is obviously a good-natured, easy-going type, but he did get a bit heated about the menace of dogs on the loose. There are more and more tourists in the area, and more and more are bringing their dogs up the glen. Untrained dogs off the leash are a menace in the countryside as well as in town, and Robbie told me that he has lost as many as nine sheep and three lambs in a week. Quite apart from killing and maiming, dogs on the rampage can ruin a long, hard day's work by scattering sheep which have just been gathered, and sometimes chase animals into the river, where they drown. Robbie has enough problems with foxes and, he claims, the occasional eagle, but he is certainly not a dog hater. His relationship with his own working dogs is a joy to observe, but he does feel very strongly that pet dogs should be more carefully controlled.

GLEN NEVIS AND MOUNTAIN MOTORING

THE ENTRY FROM THE MOOR to Glen Nevis is on open, rough ground with the huge bulk of the Ben towering over your right shoulder. As you descend, the glen narrows rapidly to a steep, tangled, rocky gorge, with rushing torrents and deep pools partly concealed by scattered boulders as big as houses. The rocky path is steep and much eroded, for it is within easy reach of the tourists who come up from Fort William, to slog part of the way up the track before turning back. At one time it was planned to dam the gorge for a hydro-electric scheme but, because of public protest, the idea was indefinitely postponed. The chances are that at some future date, the project will be sneaked back in.

There is a legend that clan Cameron, who once lived here, were guaranteed their tenancy as long as they could produce a snowball on demand at any time of the year. The Camerons would never have had much of a problem, as there are endless gullies, corries, and fields of

Glen Nevis

snow on the Ben at all times. Not content with negotiating Glen Nevis on foot, people have taken to the river Nevis itself, and there is a Glen Nevis river race once a year, a crazy event which attracts daredevils and head-bangers of all kinds, pulls great crowds of spectators and is tremendous fun. There is, however, a serious intent, which is to raise funds for the Lochaber Mountain Rescue Team, who have saved many lives on Ben Nevis and the surrounding mountains.

As on the river, much fun and enjoyment is to be had on the mountain, but there is danger and tragedy there too. At 1343 metres, the Ben has an Arctic climate in winter, and gale-force winds are commonplace. The mountain covers a vast area, and though it looks like a fairly featureless mound from most low-level viewpoints, it is a vast wilderness riven by gullies, fissures, corries and chimneys, with treacherous snow cornices and dizzying cliffs. People still wander into this other world unprepared, unfit and uninformed, though even skilled and experienced people also come to grief. A glance through the Lochaber Mountain Rescue Team's handbook illustrates the consequences of underestimating the mountain. In January 1989: two rescues. In February: eight. March: four. April: three. May: four. June: five, and so on. Some of these outings, often very hazardous for the team, result not in a rescue, but in the recovery of a body. There are several deaths each year, and a depressing statistic quoted by the rescue teams is that many more people have died on Ben Nevis than on the north face of the Eiger.

Away back in 1895, someone initiated the tradition of the Ben Nevis race and, ever since then, hardy fell runners from all over Britain have come here to test their speed and stamina against the mountain. Before the race was stopped in 1904, when the obervatory closed, an eighty-year-old man ran to the top in three hours and, to dispel any lingering doubt that he was a desperate old show-off, danced a highland fling on the observatory roof. The race was re-instated on a regular basis in 1943 and, incredibly, the time is now down to less than one and a half hours. A chap called Dave Cannon from Kendal in the English Lake District won the event no fewer than five times in the 1970s.

I have an interest in old cars, and I remember attempting to negotiate the purchase of a little pre-war, two-seater Alvis some years ago in an Edinburgh pub. The seller, a very affable lad, informed me that the car had been to the summit of Ben Nevis, and I immediately told him that I expected a substantial reduction in the price of any car which had been subjected to such abuse. More recently I interviewed David Pat Walker, an erstwhile controller of BBC Scotland. Pat delights in raking through the BBC sound archives, and he played me a wonderful recorded interview with a man called Henry Alexander who had driven a Model-T Ford to the summit in 1911. Mr Alexander and his team carefully surveyed the route, clearing boulders, widening the path, and using planks as temporary bridges. The journey was done in two stages, taking three days to the halfway mark and another two to the top. The recording made interesting listening, as Mr Alexander chatted casually about the wheels slipping to the edge of precipices of several hundred metres.

The Ben Nevis Observatory was the first mountain observatory in Europe, and began as four walls covered by a tarpaulin. This was followed by a properly equipped building which did not function for very long, closing in 1904. The summit now boasts an Ordnance Survey obelisk, and a memorial to the dead of two world wars and the victims of Hiroshima.

RESCUES, DISASTERS AND ENGLISH SCOTLAND

G LEN NEVIS YOUTH HOSTEL provides a complete contrast to
Loch Ossian. It is several times the size, very easy of access in
the heart of a popular tourist area, and is grade one hostel
standard. This means duvets, small dormitories, a common room, a
drying room, showers, a cycle store, car parking and a well-stocked
shop. It also means lots of people and, despite the hospitality, one
night there was enough for me. Malky and I were pleasantly surprised
to find that it was run by Scots, a likeable couple called Margaret and
Jimmy Adams.

Margaret told me that the size and popularity of the hostel made
for a very demanding and time-consuming job, but it was obvious that
she thrived on it. The greatest adjustment the Adamses had to make
on coming to Glen Nevis was to the consequences of being so close to
the mountain. Margaret told me that she quickly became used to
patching up minor injuries or summoning the doctor, but said that she
had to back away from one lad who was brought in, who had come off
a cliff face. His belay had held him, but when he reached the end of

Glen Nevis

the fall, the rope had swung him face first into the rock face.

She still remembers the superbly fit seventy-two-year-old man who left the hostel without informing anyone of his destination. This didn't seem to matter too much in his case, as he was a vastly experienced and able mountain man. When he failed to return, a search was mounted in the area in which his fellow hostellers thought that he had been interested. He was eventually found dead at the foot of an extensive landslide. This accident was sheer bad luck and could have happened to anyone. The man was very fit, knew his mountains, and was well-organised with planned routes, food and clothing. He just happened to be in the wrong place at the wrong time. Margaret and Jimmy later met his son and grandson, who felt that, if he had to go, this was the way – on the mountains he loved.

The incident which most impressed the Adamses concerned a boy of seventeen who went missing. He was immobilised on the mountain by a leg injury which happened at one o'clock one Monday, and was not found until noon on the Wednesday. His survival was against all the odds, and was due to his youth, determination, and the fact that he was well-clothed and equipped. He was back in his home, hale and hearty, after two weeks in hospital, where he was treated for frost-bite.

The hostel was crammed to capacity on the night we stayed, mostly with very young continentals, but I did meet one interesting character, a lady called Jeanette Barr. Jeanette is a tiny, energetic, attractive elf of a woman, whose fragile appearance belies the fact that, according to her friends, she is a wee dynamo on the hill, and has already conquered a clutch of Munros.

When we had showered and fed, Malky and I wandered down to the local café, which is run by a very friendly couple (English, of course), and there we met a couple of lads who stared at me in amazement. They explained that my book on the West Highland Way had first got them out on the route, and they could hardly believe that, at the end of 154 kilometres, I should be the first person they met. I'm glad to say that, unlike some people, they did not curse me for seducing them into an ordeal, but told me that they had enjoyed it immensely. I am reliably informed that somewhere on the rather painful Loch Lomond stretch of the West Highland Way, a suffering walker has carved into one of the marker posts the bitter message, 'Jimmie Macgregor is a blank blank blank!'

As we relaxed over our tea cups, the telly in the corner flickered into life, and we were informed that we were about to see a video about Glen Nevis. The credits rolled, and attractive scenics of the Glen followed each other as the presenter appeared. He had the obligatory beard, sweater and waxed jacket, and a nice English accent. Malky spluttered into his tea cup, leapt to his feet and vacated the premises. 'But Malky,' I protested, 'the man knows his stuff, and probably loves the place.' 'Expletive!' said Malky, as he stomped off towards the pub. My own reaction to this kind of thing is less extreme, but it does seem a trifle bizarre that people from all over the world are coming to Scotland to be told about it in English accents, to stay in English-owned hotels, and buy their souvenirs in English-owned craft shops. Perhaps the English visitors now come because they feel at home, and if they do want to meet Scots people, we could perhaps divert them to Nova Scotia or New Zealand.

FORT WILLIAM: HIGH DIVERS
AND CHARLIE'S BREEKS

I DOUBT VERY MUCH whether anyone has ever gone back to Paris, California or Tokyo raving about the beauty and charm of Fort William, but it is an important highland junction on the shore of Loch Linnhe. The Fort, as it's known, has a railway station, and the roads divide here: west for Glenfinnan and Arisaig, north for Fort Augustus and Loch Ness, and north-east to Aviemore. Most people assume that the fort dates from the Jacobite uprisings but, in fact, the first fort here was erected nearly 100 years earlier, and was built by General Monk. This was something of a chicken-wire and papier-mâché job, and was later replaced by a solid stone one which, in 1746, held out against a siege by Cameron of Lochiel, one of Bonnie Prince Charlie's more sensible officers.

When I passed through here during the making of my radio series on the West Highland Way, I spent some of the time in the West Highland Folk Museum in Cameron Square. The accent is on the old agriculture and clan life of the highlands, and the period of the Jacobite uprisings is well represented. They have an ancient pair of tartan trews here which are said to have been worn by Bonnie Prince Charlie. The breeks were obviously made of a very shrink-prone

(*Left*)
The Ferry, Fort William

(*Page 73*)
Loch Eil

material, or the Prince was an anorexic dwarf. The *pièce de résistance* is the famous 'Hidden Portrait' of Charles Edward. The painting is a cleverly arranged series of seemingly meaningless blobs and squiggles, but when a special mirrored tube is placed at the correct angle on the picture, one sees, reflected on the cylinder, a likeness of the Prince, dressed in satin and wearing a dark wig.

Our next stop was the little ferry which was to take us across Loch Linnhe. John and Hugh Haining, who run the boat, were waiting for us at the little side pier, on a grey, rainy morning. As we were about to board, I noticed a group of young people milling around on the main pier, in flippers, goggles and rubber suits weighed down with tubes, tanks, lead weights, and all the paraphernalia of people who love to submerge themselves in dark, icy Scottish lochs. 'What's it all about?' I asked Alan Ferguson. He told me that he and the other divers were members of Strathclyde University Diving Club. He further explained that they were trying to raise funds for a disabled divers' club, by taking on the highest ascent in Scotland. A laudable enterprise, but I pointed out that people were going up Ben Nevis all the time. 'Yes,' said Alan, 'and that's where we're going, but we'll start from 9 metres below the surface of Loch Linnhe.' Having wished them luck, we boarded the ferry for the short crossing. The weather was clearing, and a pleasant walk brought us to Loch Eil where we turned west for Glenfinnan and Loch Shiel.

A BREW-UP

WE WERE ENJOYING perfect bright, breezy walking weather as we made our way along the south shore of Loch Eil. Here, there were miles of sandpiper-trilling beaches, statuesque grey herons and purple foxgloves under sweeping larches. Happily removed from the human bustle just across the water, we could see where the Caledonian Canal entered Loch Linnhe, having come through the locks at Banavie. There are eight of these locks, and they can raise the level of the canal by 20 metres in one minute. Known as Neptune's Staircase, the locks are yet another splendid achievement of the Scottish civil engineer Thomas Telford.

A little further along the loch, the pulp mill at Corpach isn't quite as romantic or visually attractive and, sadly, has proven to be not as practical a proposition as the locks. But even Corpach has a story, for the name means the Place of the Corpses, and in times past the remains of the noble and great were brought here to be taken to the sacred Isle of Iona for burial.

As we passed the Loch Eil Outward Bound Centre at Achdalieu Lodge across the water, I suggested that it was time for a morning brew-up. Malky readily agreed and we were keeping our eyes open

for a place sheltered from the brisk breeze, when we saw it. A telephone box. Big, isolated, old-fashioned and bright red, the way telephone boxes should be. Totally windproof, it was the ideal place to get the stove going. With a few minor adjustments to the interior furnishings, the billy was soon bubbling nicely. The phone rang! 'Hellew,' said an extremely fruity English voice. 'Could you advise me of the price of yore stroeberrehs?' 'A pun' per punnet,' we said in unison, hung up, and carried on making the tea.

Before leaving, we tidied up the phone box and studied the Ardgour Community Council's minutes which were pinned to a board alongside our tea-room. The overall impression was that life wasn't terribly frantic along the shores of Loch Eil.

GLENFINNAN

IT WAS IN GLENFINNAN at the head of Loch Shiel, on 19 August 1745, that the young Charles Edward Stuart launched his epic, and ultimately disastrous, campaign to restore the Stuart dynasty – a dynasty which had begun with Marjorie, daughter of Robert the Bruce, and had lasted for 400 years. The Catholic Bishop Hugh McDonald blessed the venture, and the standard was raised by the Marquis of Tullibardine, already a frail old man but, like so many others, ready to sacrifice all for the Bonnie Prince. The long reign of the Stuarts, the events leading up to the rising of '45, followed by the defeat and Charles's five-month flight through the Highlands before escaping to France, are dealt with in some detail in my book, *In the Footsteps of Bonnie Prince Charlie*.

The head of Loch Shiel is one of Scotland's most popular tourist attractions, and is now in the care of the National Trust for Scotland. The well-used visitors' centre has an audio-visual display, a shop which avoids the usual excesses of tartanry, a wide selection of Scottish books, and lots of interesting information about the Prince's campaign, and about the surrounding district.

A path from the centre leads to the famous Glenfinnan monument on the loch shore. It consists of a slim tower within a walled enclosure. A narrow, circular, stone staircase takes the visitor to the top, where a huge stone figure, kilted and feather-bonneted, gazes endlessly down the waters of Loch Shiel. Many of the visitors take away

The Monument, Glenfinnan

with them the belief that this is Bonnie Prince Charlie but, in fact, the figure represents all the clansmen who fought for the Jacobite cause. The monument was raised in 1815 by MacDonald of Glenaladale, whose father had fought and died at Culloden, and it is said that some of the stones used came from cairns built by Glenfinnan men. Before going off to battle, the clansmen would add a stone to a cairn, removing it when they got back. The stones which remained represented the dead, and were placed by the dead.

Loch Shiel is a long, narrow loch snaking away south west to the sea. It is hemmed in all along its length by steep hills, heavily wooded on the lower slopes. It is totally wild and superbly beautiful, and from the little knoll behind the visitors' centre, thousands of photographs of the loch have been taken, many by me, with the monument providing a splendid focal point in the foreground.

The West Highland Railway has a station at Glenfinnan, and a little way up the glen is the famous Glenfinnan viaduct. I travelled across this on the train when I made a radio programme about the West Highland Railway. I've walked under it, and viewed it near and far from many different angles, and I never tire of it. The viaduct sweeps across the glen in a graceful crescent more than 300 metres long. The massive weight is supported by 30-metre-high pillars surmounted by arches, the whole so beautifully designed and engineered that it seems weightless, and appears to float. From far back and high up in the

Loch Shiel

glen, the sight of the seemingly tiny train puffing over the viaduct, with a trailing plume of smoke, is sheer delight. There is a story that during its construction a horse and cart broke through the planks over one of the hollow supports, to crash to the bottom 30 metres below. They are still there.

A peculiarity of the church on the little hill near the visitors' centre is that it has no bell tower. The MacDonald who built the church as a memorial to Charles Edward Stuart had invested all his money in the Vatican State. When that was amalgamated with Italy, he suddenly found himself short of funds, and mounted his bell on a little bracket at ground level.

A DISCOVERY, MARTYRS
AND MYTHS

SINCE MY LAST VISIT to Glenfinnan, a plaque has been displayed at the visitors' centre, informing the curious of a recent discovery concerning the site of the raising of Bonnie Prince Charlie's standard. Most people accept that the monument does not mark the exact position but that the standard was raised somewhere in the area. Several years ago a fire exposed some large, flat stones on the little hill above the Catholic church, and in 1988 an article appeared in the

Scots Magazine which set out to prove that this was the authentic site of the standard ceremony. It was written by Ian Thomson, who is now Highland Regional Councillor for Ardnamurchan. Mr Thomson had made a careful study of the stones, and his article caused quite a stir among Scottish historians and antiquarians. There are inscriptions which purport to show the positions of the principal figures during the ceremony, and carved footprints mark the stances taken by the aged Tullibardine and the Prince himself.

The interest and excitement generated by the discovery and the claims made for it are easy to understand. There is a well-known painting by Skeoch Cumming of the standard-raising, and the surroundings depicted certainly match up more closely to the recently discovered site than to the ones on the flat foreshore. However, it must be remembered that Cumming painted his picture long after the event, and Ronnie MacKellaig, who is of an old local family and is now in charge of the visitors' centre, is convinced Skeoch Cumming had never been to Glenfinnan. Moreover, Ronnie told me that local tradition, passed down through the old folk, locates another site further up the glen, and that's not the only one. The stones are on private ground, and the local priest has been objecting to folk tramping through it. The National Trust for Scotland acknowledges the interest in the theory, but does not accept the evidence as conclusive and visitors are discouraged.

The exact location of the standard-raising may never be known, but it is surely enough that somewhere here was enacted one of the most glamorous and dramatic ceremonies in Scottish history. The day started badly, for the Prince sailed up Loch Shiel to find only a few MacDonalds awaiting him, and there was a long, frustrating wait before the distant sound of the pipes heralded the approach of about 800 of clan Cameron, with the young Lochiel at their head. This was deemed enough for the ceremony to begin, and the situation improved still further as more and more support continued to arrive. McDonnell of Keppoch brought about 300 men; a group of McLeods from Skye presented themselves, in defiance of their unsympathetic chief, and soon the glen was loud with the skirl of the pipes, and the excited shouts and cries of well over 1000 exultant, optimistic clansmen. What we feel now in Glenfinnan is the sadness of a lost cause, and a way of life which had gone beyond its time, and was inevitably doomed.

The mythology persists, and if one takes care not to examine the facts too closely, the story is wonderfully romantic and dramatic. A handsome, gallant young leader, great displays of courage, sacrifice and fealty; and a thoroughly bad baddie in the shape of the Duke of Cumberland, conveniently corpulent and unattractive. However, facts are chiels that winna ding*, and there were Lowlanders and Highlanders on both sides at Drummossie Moor. Only one of the three chieftains in Skye lent Charlie his support, and many of the clan chiefs decided not to be involved; some from conviction, others from self-interest. It was Cumberland's brutality after Culloden, and his subsequent rape of the Highlands, that made martyrs of the Jacobites and helped create the myth.

LOCH SHIEL: JOLLY BOATING WEATHER

W E WERE NOW HEADING for Ardnamurchan, and the last stages of our journey across Scotland. The country here is extremely wild and rugged, and at one time the only way people could travel along the peninsula was by boat. We decided to go the same way. Our boatman was Donald Macaulay, known as Dee; a quiet, courteous man, fair-haired and lean-jawed. His boat was rather wee. Producer Dennis Dick is rather large, and in addition to Malky and myself there were Barry and Bob with camera and tape recorder. The little boat was totally exposed to the weather, which, on the day of our journey, was the worst we had encountered since we left Montrose. The downpour was solid and remained so all day. Visibility was virtually nil on what would have been one of the most spectacularly scenic parts of the whole journey. To add to the fun, a crocodile, cleverly disguised as a midge, had attacked my nose, swelling the bridge so that I had to bend over to see round it. However, it was Malky's birthday, and we put all aside for a small impromptu celebration, while Barry filmed away in the worst possible conditions.

All in all, things weren't going too badly. One always tends to make entertainment out of these impossible situations and we were having a few laughs. We became almost hysterical with merriment

---

* *chiels that winna ding* = the truth cannot be denied

With Dee on Loch Shiel

when the engine coughed, hesitated, spluttered apologetically, and finished the shift. I have never really believed in the internal combustion engine, so I wasn't surprised – but I was a little concerned. We were sitting in a relentless downpour in the middle of a remote loch in the middle of remote country. We were about halfway down the 14 kilometres to our destination at Dalilea. There was no road or track on our side even if we could get to shore. Dee obviously had more faith in his engine than I have in any engine, for there were no oars on board. We solved this problem by unscrewing bits of the boat, and with Dennis sculling at the stern using the centre seat as an oar and Malky and me paddling with a couple of metal panels, we inched slowly and painfully towards a rocky, tangled shore. The map showed one tiny, isolated cottage about two kilometres back, and after tying up with some difficulty, Malky was elected to leg it along for help. A man called Tony Millard lives there in splendid isolation, and by sheer good luck was accepting callers that day. On the previous day he had been away in Glasgow for provisions. With Tony's help, we were soon under way again, and arrived in Dalilea very late, taiglet* and drookit*, but grateful.

---

* *taiglet* = harassed   * *drookit* = drenched, soaked

The guest house at Dalilea is run by Dee's wife and his two charming daughters, Eilidh and Mhairi. We were soon dry and warm, and settling down to a grand meal, the events of the day becoming more preposterous and comical as we re-hashed them. Despite the poor visibility, the trip down Loch Shiel had been interesting. We were always aware that Bonnie Prince Charlie had sailed up these very waters on the way to the start of his great adventure. This is a truly wild and isolated area, and the haunt of fox, badger, eagle and pine marten. We were lucky enough to catch good sightings of a couple of black-throated divers, with their wonderfully intricate markings. I bragged to Malky that I had once won a medal for a drawing of the bird, but didn't mention that it was when I was eleven years old.

Just before arriving at Dalilea, we passed Eilean Fhianain, Finnan's Isle, with its chapel and burial ground. Saint Finnan came here in the sixth century, bringing with him, it is said, a bell with healing powers. The bell is still there, and in the ancient burial ground lie the bodies of generations of local people. Catholics and Protestants demonstrated their traditional Christian tolerance by ensuring that even the dead were segregated, with a part of the cemetery for Catholic corpses, and another for reformed remains. St Finnan was one of many Irish missionaries who came to Scotland, and his beloved Eilean Uaine, 'The Green Isle', long rivalled St Columba's Iona as a holy place. The famous bell, which is of cast bronze, was rung to herald the arrival of funeral parties from across the loch. The mourners would then circle the chapel three times in the direction of the sun. The island was for centuries the burial place of the MacDonalds of Clanranald. Many of the ancient Scottish coffin roads led to the shores of Loch Shiel, where the deceased ended their journey on a funeral barge. Some of the old routes taken by pall-bearers and mourners can still be traced in the surrounding hills.

ARDNAMURCHAN: SALMON AND STRONTIUM

IN THE SPLENDID Glasgow Garden Festival of 1988, there was a fine exhibition called 'Ardnamurchan, Almost an Island', and that is an almost perfect description of an almost perfect place. The long oval shape of the Ardnamurchan peninsula lies to the south-

Postbox, Acharacle

west of Moidart, and north of Morvern and the Isle of Mull. It is joined to the mainland at the Sunart end only by a narrow neck of land between Kentra Bay near Acharacle, and Salen, to the south on the shore of Loch Sunart. Ardnamurchan is approximately 19 kilometres from end to end, but the only viable road twists, dips and winds along the southern coast, with one little loop inland before continuing westwards to the sea.

The name Ardnamurchan is from the Gaelic, Ard na Mór Chuainn, which means 'The Point, or Heights of the Seas'. There is evidence of human habitation here from as far back as the Stone Age, with a chambered cairn from that period at Kilchoan, standing stones from the Bronze Age, and reminders of the Celts of the Iron Age in several hill forts. The influence of the Norsemen who held sway here for so long is still present in many of the place names of the west coast and its islands. The long rule of the Vikings was finally brought to an end by one Iain Sprangach, which could be translated as 'Iain the rather pushy', as he then appointed himself Lord of Ardnamurchan.

The Lordship of the Isles passed in time to the MacDonalds, who were all-powerful for a long period, and administered much of the west coast and the islands as their own personal kingdom. Not everyone was pleased by this arrangement, and their power was eventually broken, King James IV accepting their submission at Mingarry Castle in 1495. The castle is now a dramatic ruin a little to the east of

Kilchoan, on the south shore. In 1664, it was captured by the followers of Montrose; and it was here, in 1745, that Campbell of Achinduin became the first official to hear of the landing in Scotland of the young pretender, Prince Charles Edward Louis John Sylvester Maria Casimir Stuart, better known as BPC.

The road into Ardnamurchan follows the north shore of Loch Sunart, where there has been much development of fish farming. In my book, *In the Footsteps of Bonnie Prince Charlie*, I spoke of the changes wrought in the Scottish countryside by this recent activity, and of the benefits and the problems. On Loch Sunart, when I was there, problems seemed to be predominating, and there was much talk of people losing their jobs. Naturalists and conservationists have been worried for some time about some of the side effects of fish farming.

It is obvious that any creature which preys upon fish is the fish farmer's enemy, and seals and, it is claimed, herons, even ospreys, have already fallen victim. The greatest worry, leaving aside aesthetic considerations, is the effect of the farming on other sea life. Unused, downward-drifting food can cause pollution, and the chemicals used to combat health problems, such as sea lice, among the closely packed fish, have been shown to damage or kill creatures ranging from mussels to lobsters.

The most serious problem is that local authorities have no power in decisions concerning fish farming. The sites are leased by the Crown Estates, and the fact that their representatives are unelected and appear to answer to no one but themselves, gives great cause for concern. Everyone, conservationists included, can see the advantages of any new industry in the Highlands, with the potential for employment and much-needed economic stimulus, but the general feeling is that anything as important as fish farming should be more open to discussion by the people whom it affects, and much more carefully regulated than it appears to be.

At the far eastern end of Loch Sunart, however, a discovery was made in the eighteenth century which reduces the problems of fish farming to insignificance. The Campbells, who held the Ardnamurchan estates until 1723, were bought out by one Alexander Murray, who first opened the lead mines at Strontian. They were worked by the Duke of Norfolk and then by the York mining company. Most of the several hundred employees were Irish and it was a very profitable concern until its closure in 1740. Some time later, a mineral called strontianite was found, and mining began again for this and barytes, or barium sulphate, used in white paints. From strontianite, the element strontium was identified and isolated and mankind was on its way to another giant leap backwards with the invention of the atomic bomb. Barytes is still mined in the area, by a firm from England.

THE KIRK ON THE WATER

IN THE MIDDLE of the last century, the people of Ardnamurchan were having trouble with a very autocratic landowner called James Riddell. Riddell was an incomer, a lowlander of the Episcopalian persuasion who regarded the adherence of the local folk to the Free Kirk as something akin to devil worship, and an affront to Queen and country. He did everything in his power – which was almost absolute – to make life difficult for those who would not toe his, and the establishment's, line and flatly refused permission for a church anywhere on his vast estates. It was probably true of the adherents of the Free Church that they were as intolerant as many other religious groups, but they did have a valid and serious grievance.

The Patronage Act of 1712 conferred on the lairds the absolute right to appoint their own parish ministers, and as the minister at that time was a powerful figure with great authority over his flock, he could be a very useful tool for social and political control. Ian Crichton Smith's book, *Consider the Lilies*, gives an example of the attitudes and effect of a lick-spittle minister during the clearance evictions. The Free Church claimed that the Patronage Act broke the rules of the Treaty of Union of 1707, but the Treaty was a *fait accompli*, and Queen Anne and her ministers in Westminster could do as they pleased. What they pleased was to empower the gentry to appoint parish ministers who would do what they were told, and force the people to do likewise.

When three legitimate representatives of the Free Kirk were completely cold-shouldered on an attempt to petition the Queen and her ministers in London, the Ardnamurchan folk came up with an ingenious solution. In a Clydeside shipyard, a complete church was built on a flat-bottomed iron barge. It was 8 metres high, 24 metres long and 7 metres across, and could accommodate 400 people. There was a precentor's desk, a vestry and a pulpit, and in 1846 the whole caboodle could have been seen moving majestically up Loch Sunart, with the help of two steam tugs.

The barge was securely anchored in a bay near Strontian, and under the baleful eye of the frustrated Riddell, business began. Free Kirk worshippers from all over Ardnamurchan turned up, to get into small boats and haul themselves over on fixed lines. The church was said to sink 2.5 centimetres lower for each 100 people, and the minister's popularity could be judged by the level of the waterline. Ventilation was bad, the weather was sometimes rough on the loch, and there was no place to pee, but the Ardnamurchan folk were happy, and Riddell was put in his place.

ACHARACLE AND OCKLE
TO KILCHOAN

A RDNAMURCHAN WAS NEW territory to me, and although its basic character is under threat from the influences of incomers, it is still beautiful and interesting; a wonderful place which I shall certainly revisit, perhaps in a more leisurely fashion. At Acharacle we called in to see Fergie MacDonald, who runs a popular bar and restaurant. Fergie is a kenspeckle* figure in Ardnamurchan, and indeed all over Scotland, for he is one of our veteran Scottish-dance musicians, and a wizard on the accordion, squeeze box, or mangle. Fergie's music features fairly regularly on my daily radio programme.

Acharacle is named for the battle of Ath Tharracaill, which means Torquil's Ford. Torquil was a Viking lord in the twelfth century, and his adversary at Acharacle was Somerled, one of Scotland's great early chieftains. From the splendid bridge which now replaces the ford, Malky and I paused to watch a pair of mergansers riding the current with consummate skill. We were now heading for a wee place called Arivegaig, and the old footpath over to Ockle.

As we set off, we were aware of the countless people who had passed this way before us, for the track was an important route

* *kenspeckle* = well-known, familiar

The path for Ockle

through the peninsula, connecting several small settlements. We had started off in poor, but tolerable weather, and as we were almost at the highest point of the track, the sun began to blink through, to light up a fine scene behind us. Above the path and to our right was Suidhe Fhinain, Finnan's Seat, a large split stone from which St Finnan first caught sight of his beloved Eilean Uaine on distant Loch Shiel. From the same vantage point, we could look back to Kentra Bay and the famous 'Singing Sands'. The singing is an odd whining or moaning sound caused by the friction of the grains of sand. The sand is gleamingly, beautifully white, but always on the move, and beneath its pristine surface lie the buildings of a settlement which was totally swallowed up.

As we crossed the high point and began to descend, we moved off the path and up on to a sort of escarpment which gave us a superb view out to sea. The sky was now brilliantly blue with the merest wisps of cloud, and the distant white horses rode over a sea of ultramarine and emerald, in places almost purple. Before us lay Eigg, with its well-known Sgurr, the mountain at the south end which gives the island its rather odd profile. To the south of Eigg, the much smaller island of

First glimpse of the islands

Muck, which caused us so much merriment at school; and beyond Eigg, the much more imposing bulk of Rum, its grand blue peaks concealing, from this angle, the little island of Canna. I had spent some time on Rum while filming my television series on islands, and I was able to tell Malky about the reintroduction of the magnificent sea eagle to the island, and thence to the west of Scotland. I was glad to see that as we approached the end of our journey, Malky was becoming quite a bird man.

We were now heading for Kilchoan, the so-called capital of Ardnamurchan, and still enjoying the views out to sea, as we made our way down towards Swordle and Kilmory. In a splendid book called *Discovering Argyll, Mull and Iona*, shepherd-turned-historian Willie Orr tells us that in 1829 there were fifteen families living at Kilmory, with about the same number nearby. Today, there are only about six crofts, with a few sheep but no cows. These are mostly occupied by elderly people, and there are very few children, a situation to be found all over the Highlands. At one time, Scottish glens, now described by enthusiastic visitors as superb wilderness worth preserving, supported healthy populations, and the wilderness was enriched by cattle, not stripped by sheep or deer.

ALASDAIR MAC MHAIGHSTIR
ALASDAIR

KILMORY WAS FOR A TIME the home of a man outstanding even among that special breed, the Highland minister. He was Alasdair Mac Mhaighstir Alasdair, born around 1700 (the exact date is not known). Hugh McDairmid called him by far the greatest of all the great Gaelic poets, and his wife called him 'Muideartach dubh dana geur-fhacal'; in English, 'the bold, black Moidartman of the sharp words'. The author Ronald Black, who has made a study of Alasdair, describes him as a literary colossus inviting comparison with the world's greatest. He taught at Kilmory school for about seven years. The title Mhaighstir, or master, identified the holder of a university degree, and was commonly used for priests and ministers.

Alasdair was a man of diverse and extraordinary abilities. In 1741, when in the employ of a group called the Society in Scotland for the Propagation of Christian Knowledge, he produced a dictionary known as a *Galick and English Vocabulary*. The official policy of the group was 'the reformation of the highlands and islands and other places where popery and ignorance abound'. This enlightened team started off by banning the teaching and use of Latin and Gaelic in Highland schools, and Alasdair's dictionary was the result of the discovery that Highland children were capable of reciting great chunks of scripture in English, without understanding a single syllable.

Alasdair's literary output was prodigious, and this was while he was teaching and ministering to his flock, but he was no stuffy academic, or prissy aesthete. Even among the hardy people of Sunart and Ardnamurchan, he was known for his physique and stamina, and, when preaching in Kilchoan, would regularly walk there and back from Dalilea in the same day. This is an almost incredible journey of 80 kilometres or so, over the most forbidding terrain. He was a real hero even to those who disagreed with him, and for a minister his language and style could be rather robust. He warned his parishioners in a very straightforward way about the dangers of 'an Clapa', the venereal disease which had been introduced to the peninsula by the Strontian miners. When two local men aged seventy were found to be indulging in a bit of wandering womanising, Alasdair chastised them in verse which translates from Gaelic as:

The old bulls are as randy
As well-equipped three-year-olds
And though good is the grass of the corries,
Seven times better is the grass of Fascadale.

He could also turn a very fine insult, as here, again in translation:

You've a hedgehog's visage, a boar's belly face,
The bone-raven's bosom and the nature of the pig,
The mouth of the catfish and the badger's stench,
Splay feet, heels full of kibes,
The legs of a heron, the lobster's breast,
Festering, scaly, watering eyes –
With inches of Bardic satire
I measure you from your brow to your heel
and I flay your hide, you slave, off you
Because you have defamed Black Campbell.

UNSETTLING SETTLERS

NEAR KILCHOAN is the impressive pile of Glenborrodale Castle, in its extensive wooded policies. It was built in 1902 by one Charles Rudd, who demolished a perfectly respectable house to make way for his rather more flamboyant dwelling. It was built with imported stone which actually looks slightly odd in the surroundings, and it has passed through several ownerships since Rudd died in 1916. It is, at the time of writing, the property of Mr Peter de Savary, who runs it as an up-market, sixteen-bedroomed hotel, with attractions like yachting, bird watching, bird killing, sauna sweating, and solarium scorching. I hear very good reports of it. Mr de Savary also owns a well-known gambling establishment in London, and a chunk of an independent TV station. Land's End is his, as is John o' Groats. Obviously a very interesting and influential character, and I was looking forward to my arranged meeting with him at the Ardnamurchan lighthouse complex. Yes, he owns that too. This means that Mr de Savary has possession of the most southerly, northerly and westerly parts of Great Britain, and only needs some place like Lowestoft to make up the set.

I recently read a newspaper article about the island of Arran, one of the beloved haunts of my youth. The writer quite properly extolled the beauties and attractions of the island, and described it as Scotland in miniature, with woods and rivers, rugged mountain country with splendid peaks and ridges to the north, and at the south, more gentle agricultural land. What she did not mention was that Arran is now an English island in Scotland, with incomers comprising more than half of the population. Arran is within easy reach of Glasgow. Kilchoan, far out on a remote highland peninsula, has the same problem. Allan Mac Lachlan is the piermaster at Kilchoan, and a descendant of people who have crofted in Ardnamurchan for generations. He is a most affable and good-natured man, who would wish no one harm, but he sees the situation as very serious, with local language and ways dying a fast but not easy death.

The north/south economic divide is at the root of the problem, and the standing joke is that you sell a two-roomed bungalow in Sevenoaks and buy an estate in Scotland. Local people can't compete with prices offered when properties do come on the market, and the young people have to move away from home to live. Many of the people buying up Scottish properties have taken retirement, early or otherwise. It goes without saying that people who are prepared to uproot themselves at fifty, sixty or seventy are by definition dynamic and energetic, and tend to exercise a disproportionate influence on a small community. Some of the effects of these influences are positive, of course, and there are at least a couple of examples in Kilchoan, but as more and more older people move in, pushing out locals of mar-riageable age, there are fewer and fewer children, the schools close and the village or small town becomes little more than a sort of retiral home.

The oft-proffered argument that there are many Scots in England is a weak one. There are five million Scots and fifty million English, and the fact is that Scots go to England because they need money, and the English can move to Scotland because they have it. The situation is already widespread and serious. There are no controls, and while it is said that market forces must rule, one can look to other small countries where positive discrimination is exercised in favour of the natives, and limits are applied to the amounts of land and property which can be acquired by any individual. Oh, and by the way, some of my best friends, etc. . .

CURSE AT KILCHOAN

A LLAN MAC LACHLAN took me up to the old ruined church on a little hill near his house. The ancient stones are gradually being prised apart by the roots of plants, and one feels that the building should at least be stabilised as a ruin, the earliest parts of which go back to the thirteenth century. I am always intrigued by old graveyards, and there are some really ancient stones here. Within a railed enclosure is a much more modern stone to the memory of one John McColl, a man notorious in Ardnamurchan and Sunart for the enthusiasm with which he carried out his master's dirty work at the time of the clearances. McColl was employed as a tacksman, and one of his tasks was to evict a man with a sick wife and six children. The family saw their home destroyed and lived on the shore for six weeks before the wife died. Before she succumbed, she cursed McColl, telling him that no grass would ever grow on his grave. According to the local people, no grass did, and the rather grand, flat stone, placed by relatives from overseas, could be a gesture of defiance in the face of local people, or a cover for nettles and dockens.

Allan Mac Lachlan

Ardnamurchan suffered terribly in the clearances, when people were being thrown off the land to make way for sheep. In September 1837 twenty families left Ardnamurchan on board the ship *Brilliant*, and as the familiar peak of Ben Hiant faded from sight, they knew that they would never see their homes and loved ones again. *The Inverness Courier* of 11 October 1837 reported:

> *A large body of emigrants sailed from Tobermory on 27 September for New South Wales. The vessel was the* Brilliant, *and its size and splendid fittings were greatly admired. The people to be conveyed by this vessel are decidedly the most valuable that have ever left the shores of Great Britain. They are of excellent moral character, and from their knowledge of agriculture and management of sheep and cattle, must prove a most valuable acquisition to a colony like New South Wales.*

In their own country, sheep were more valuable.

Before the final, very short stage of our coast-to-coast walk, we had a very pleasant interlude at the Kilchoan House Hotel, which is run by Alan Mews and his wife. Alan is from the south and is well-liked locally. He seems to be making a genuine effort to adjust, even to the extent of learning a little Gaelic. He is obviously fond of the place and appears to be fitting in quite well. Perhaps it's because, as a Geordie, he's an honorary Scotsman already.

CLIMAX: BILLY AND BOLLINGER

WE ARRIVED AT OUR finishing point by the lighthouse in bright, sunlit weather to find the outlook from Ardnamurchan Point quite breathtaking. Malky, the eternal enthusiast, had run out of superlatives, and we simply soaked-in the scene. To the north-west, over a deep blue, white-speckled sea, lay the islands of Muck, Eigg and Rum, with Canna visible behind. The more distant outlines of Barra, South Uist and Benbecula were quite clearly visible, while to the north we could pick out the high tops of the Cuillins of Skye. We could not have wished for a better end to what had been a truly splendid journey across Scotland, and we celebrated in the only way we knew how. We produced the stove, the billy can, and the tea.

Peter de Savary with lightkeeper Laurie Colquhoun and Reginald Lacon of the
Northern Lighthouse Board

The lighthouse at Ardnamurchan Point was, like the one at Scurdie Ness, a product of the Stevenson family's talent. It was built in 1849 by Alan Stevenson, the uncle of Robert Louis. The tower is 35 metres high and its position on the headland raises its 550 000 candlepower light to 55 metres above the sea. The structure looks quite impregnable, but in 1852 it was struck by lightning and sustained some internal damage. Giant waves swept away 12 metres of the approach road, while 15 metres of the surrounding wall was also demolished. The lighthouse keepers had taken the precaution of tying up their boat 5 metres above the highest known watermark, but this too was smashed to bits by the storm.

I was rather disappointed that Peter de Savary didn't turn up by helicopter. He arrived by car, dead on time, and accompanied by his extremely charming wife, and moderately charming dog. He was, in some ways, what I had expected. Affable, polite and helpful, and very self-contained. Obviously a man used to quietly handling all kinds of situations. What did surprise me was his physical presence. Not too tall, but robustly constructed, he suggested more the outdoor man of action than a boardroom wimp, and slightly rakish too, in a stylish track suit and ponytail hair tied back with a little blue circlet. First of all he told me that, though he had bought the ground and ancillary buildings, he did not own the tower itself, as it was still a functioning lighthouse. I was puzzled as to why he would want a place like this, and asked him what he intended to do with it. 'Very little,' he said. 'It's so beautiful, why change it?' But he did explain that he planned to convert the rather stark buildings into cottages for holiday letting.

The people living on the peninsula have been agitating for some time for a decent road to join up with the one to Fort William. I asked Mr de Savary what he thought of the idea, and whether he might even help. He thought the idea was nonsense. Not many people wanted it, he felt, and it wouldn't save all that much travelling time. I asked him how often he used Concorde. He took this bit of cheek in good part. Allan Mac Lachlan and many others feel that a reasonable road is essential if this area is to survive as anything other than a tourists' and incomers' retreat. The local folk shop in Fort William, or take the ferry over to Tobermory on the Isle of Mull, but the ferry operates only in summer, which means a long, tortuous road journey in winter

The foghorn, Ardnamurchan Point

Looking north from Ardnamurchan Point

conditions, and there are threats that the Tobermory ferry is to be taken out of service altogether. Like Peter de Savary, I'd like to see Ardnamurchan remaining wild and beautiful, but I don't have to live there on a day-to-day, year-to-year basis. Nor can I drop in by helicopter when I feel like it.

When Mr de Savary had taken his leave, producer Dennis Dick surprised and delighted us by producing a bottle of champagne, taking the shine off Malky's billy can. There was a little round of excusable self-congratulation, I said my last piece to camera, and with a last, lingering look at the magical islands floating on a hazy blue sea, we turned our faces for home.

Ardnamurchan Light